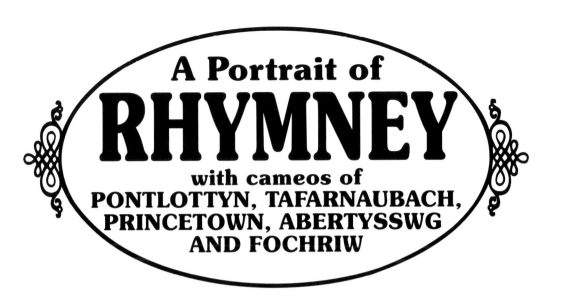

A Portrait of
RHYMNEY
with cameos of
PONTLOTTYN, TAFARNAUBACH, PRINCETOWN, ABERTYSSWG AND FOCHRIW

by Marion Evans

Volume 4

Foreword by
ROY NOBLE, BBC Wales

Old Bakehouse Publications

Abertillery

First published in December 1998

ISBN 1 874538 02 6

Published in the U.K. by
Old Bakehouse Publications
Church Street,
Abertillery, Gwent NP3 lEA
Telephone: 01495 212600 Fax: 01495 216222

Made and printed in the UK
by J.R. Davies (Printers) Ltd.

Foreword
by Roy Noble, BBC Wales

"Where am I going ?". Now there's a question that's often raised by many an individual in this fast-moving, complex and overly sophisticated world. "What's it all about ?" is another query raised by many a perplexed mind in this day and age. However, if you visit St. Catherine's House in London, the records' centre for births, marriages and deaths, then clearly you realise that two other questions are also in the mind. So many people are to be seen seeking out their past and pedigree that the reflex questions must be "Who am I ?" and 'Where have I come from?". The quest for "roots" is a very real search and the need for "belonging" is a powerful one within each soul.

Marion Evans, in this book, provides a helpful guide along that searching trail. In her profiles of Rhymney, human and otherwise, and in the shorter cameos of Tafarnaubach, Princetown, Abertysswg, Pontlottyn and Fochriw she weaves colourful patches that make up this regional valley quilt within Wales. Her photographs and text touch upon the memory and bring to life the images which are flashbacks of who we were and from where we came.

I live in another valley, the Cynon, and Aberdare is my home. My spiritual root, however, is further west in the anthracite belt of another valley, the Amman in east Carmarthenshire. Yet there is an affinity across this entire region. We are all "comers in" to an extent, our forebears answering the Klondike call to the iron, the tin and the coal. Their world was one of the early "melting pots" of the industrial revolution. They came from everywhere to form the "new" Silures tribe - the valley South Walian.

What a warm welcoming breed we still are. Those qualities, though, were nurtured by those who came before us and by the places they created and in which they lived.

"Who am I ?', "Where am I from ?". For those who live in Rhymney and the villages around, Marion Evans provides an answer and what a lovely, evocative mural it is.

Roy Noble

Contents

FOREWORD

INTRODUCTION

CHAPTER 1   IN AND AROUND RHYMNEY

CHAPTER 2   TRADE & INDUSTRY

CHAPTER 3   RELIGION & CHOIRS

CHAPTER 4   EDUCATION & SPORT

CHAPTER 5   PEOPLE & EVENTS

CHAPTER 6   TAFARNAUBACH & PRINCETOWN

CHAPTER 7   ABERTYSSWG

CHAPTER 8   PONTLOTTYN

CHAPTER 9   FOCHRIW

Introduction

History is too often written in terms of dates, Royal Houses, nations and empires. I believe, however, that people are more important than governments and states and volume four of 'A Portrait of Rhymney' continues my theme, set in previous volumes, of being about people - our people - who lived in this small corner of an ever-changing world.

For centuries the local early hill farmer and his family lived a strenuous but generally settled lifestyle save for the occasional threat of incursion from the south. He was self-supporting, capable of undertaking a considerable wealth of craftwork and enjoyed trading his goods at the local fairs and markets. Then, two hundred years ago, arrived the English industrialists who gained great wealth from their exploitation of the rich mineral deposits that lay below hill and valley floor. They provided work, housing, religious and social facilities to a flood of immigrants who came to work in their furnaces and mines, but they also brought a grief and horror to a struggling workforce that was unprecedented in the history of the area. We saw starving miners and their children as everyday events, deaths and mutilation in blast furnace and coalmine, the horror of cholera epidemics and families living in poverty in tiny overcrowded cottages.

This is a book about those people, real people, who lived through those years. It is about their personalities, their eccentricities and their community spirit. It is about their courage in rising above their environment to produce famous poets, musicians and singers that rivalled the world. As well as providing day to day information about their way of life, complemented by lots of photographs, I have included a selection of biographical studies and have tried to capture the human element, as well as the pathos, of the times. My sincere thanks are extended to the many people who have kindly loaned photographs for this volume and to those who have allowed me to pick their brains for snippets of fascinating information about the past.

My special thanks are also extended to Roy Noble for kindly preparing the foreword for this volume. Roy is acutely aware of the inter-woven past that exists between communities of the South Wales coalfield and the need to sustain a memory of the people who lived through those times. His popularity as a television and radio presenter and as an author has brought a great deal of pleasure to a great number of people and I am privileged to have received his support.

It is my dearest hope that the reader will be able to walk through the streets of Rhymney and her surrounding villages with new eyes, widened from the insight into their past that I have tried to preserve through my 'portraits'.

Last, but not least, I wish to thank Roy, my dear husband, for his constant support and his positive and valuable advice without which this book would not have been written.

Volume four of 'A Portrait of Rhymney'
is hereby dedicated to my mother, father, uncle Dai
and my dear sister Patricia.

Marion Evans.

CHAPTER 1
In and around Rhymney

1066 saw the arrival of William the Conquerer and the beginning of the age of feudalism in the country, but although his victory at Hastings made him King of England it gave William no rights over the Welsh. This did not stop him, however, from giving land to his barons on the Welsh border, the Marches, with permission to seize what they could and this they did through invasion routes along the fertile southern plains and up the Severn, Wye, Usk and Rhymney valleys. The Welsh chieftains were at the time too engrossed in dealing with their own divisive problems and intrigue to offer any co-ordinated resistance to the insurgent Normans and some even went as far as to join them in battle against each other. Such a battle took place at Blaen Rhymni when Caradog, a North Wales chieftain, conspired with the Normans to overthrow the local ruler Meredyth ap Owen and 'slew him upon the river of Rympyn' in 1072. Welsh resistance was then to increase against the Normans with many fierce battles being fought to keep them at bay and, although the Normans were well established with castles at Newport, Cardiff and Caerphilly, they never entirely commanded the hill country areas which they entered with great trepidation. The indigent Silures in areas such as Rhymney therefore generally preserved their way of life, at the same time paying tribute to the first Norman Lord of Glamorgan, Robert Fitzhamon. Known as part of the Welshry, the northern end of the Rhymney Valley was never to become the Norman-English type of manorial estate that was to be seen further south. Although plundering raids and skirmishes were to frequently take place between Norman adventurers and the native Welsh, and although much bloodshed decimated their numbers, the local mainly pastoral population continued to live a semi-independent existence and avoided much of the persecution experienced by the native Welsh who lived nearer the Norman settlements. There, for instance, the Welsh language was forbidden and natives had either to learn and speak French or, as 'traitors', become outlawed. Slavery of the Welsh was commonplace and cattle and sheep were readily confiscated. From their retreat in the hills the Silures chieftains, year after year, were engaged in revolt against the Norman oppression. One such heroic chieftain was Ivor Bach who, in 1158, gained lasting fame by raiding Cardiff Castle and kidnapping the Earl of Gloucester and his family, keeping them as prisoners, reportedly in Castell Coch, until the terms that he demanded were met. The upper Rhymney Valley continued to be a potential centre of revolt against the southern Norman Lordship and played a major role in the course of Welsh history with the uprising of Llewellyn the Last in the thirteenth century. Llewellyn, recognised as Prince of Wales, gathered his forces and stormed Caerphilly Castle in 1270 and begun a series of events which was to contribute to the downfall of the Norman stranglehold. Our local predecessors, the mettlesome Silurian tribesmen, unconquered in their hillside retreats, had long awaited such a national leader to unite the Welsh against their Norman enemies and readily took up arms in support. From this time forth the Norman influence in Wales weakened only to be replaced by the bitterly resented English infiltration and the loss of Welsh independence. So began another epoch of oppression, the infringement of Welsh privileges and the inevitable rebellion that would follow.

It was not until 1536, with the passing of the Act of Union, when Welshman Henry Tudor became King Henry VII that the old laws against the Welsh people were put to an end and Welshmen were to have the same rights and privileges as Englishmen. These changes allowed for leading Welsh nobles, as well as political opportunists, to accumulate lands and build up large estates and to enter into arranged dynastic marriages. It was in this manner that great landowners such as the Thomases, Morgans, Lewises, Butes, Beauforts, Pritchards and Herberts came into recognition.

1. Butetown took its name from John Crichton-Stuart, fifth earl and second Marquess of Bute and seventh Earl of Dumfries, K.T. who, until his death in 1848, was one of the largest landowners in South Wales. The impressively aristocratic Bute lineage goes back before 1510 at which time Sir Richard Herbert, the natural son of the first Earl of Pembroke, succeeded into the estate. Within the hereditary line, through birth and marriage, we see such names as Anne, the sister of Catherine Parr, wife of King Henry VIII, Lord Jeffreys, the son of 'Judge Jeffreys' and Lady Charlotte Windsor. John, the second Marquess of Bute, was responsible for the construction of the West Bute Dock Cardiff in 1839 which allowed the export of coal to be enhanced from the valleys' coalfield at a time of increasing supply and demand.

His land holdings locally were leased to English industrialists who took full advantage of the almost limitless mineral wealth that was available and his name was synonymous with the industrial growth of Rhymney through the construction of the Bute Ironworks in 1825 and the building of Bute Terrace in Pontlottyn (then Lower Rhymney). His son John Patrick Crichton Stuart, the third Marquess of Bute, was born in 1847, a year before his father's death, and inherited the vast wealth and estates in South Wales and Scotland left by his father. He went on, in 1875, to completely rebuild the 12th Century Castell Coch which by then had been reduced to only the ruins of its foundations. He was also responsible for the restoration of Cardiff Castle and the uncovering of the Greyfriars and Blackfriars Homes in Cardiff.

2. Sir Godfrey Morgan (1831-1913) who was raised to the peerage in 1905 to become the 2nd Baron, 1st Viscount, Tredegar. The Morgan family, until 1951, had been living at Tredegar House, Newport since the early 15th century but their family name goes back to at least the Norman Conquest. Theirs is one of the oldest family seats in Wales and Tredegar takes its name (Teigr ap Tegonwy) from, supposedly, one of the knights of Arthur's round table. The Morgan estates ranged widely throughout Wales, Scotland and England and their land locally extended eastwards from the Rhymney River whereas the Butes owned land on the west bank. The Morgans were responsible for the promoting of coal mines and ironworks on their land and the town of Tredegar was given their ancestral name when an ironworks was built there on land leased to three enterprising ironmasters in the early 19th century. They constructed canals and tramways throughout Monmouthshire and made substantial profits from the Tolls which were imposed throughout their estates.

3. The above photograph shows Sir Godfrey Morgan at Fochriw where he laid the foundation stone for St Mary's Church in 1907. Sir Godfrey, who had survived The Charge of the Light Brigade in 1854, was a highly respected public benefactor. He was created a Viscount in 1905 and made Freeman of both Cardiff and Newport in 1909.

4. The Beaufort Inn, Rhymney Bridge, which received its name from the most noble Henry, Duke of Beaufort. The Beauforts, within their vast estates, have owned the land to the north of Rhymney for hundreds of years and had always regarded themselves as the dominant political and social force in South Wales. Their lineage descends as far back as John of Gaunt, the Duke of Lancaster, whose great granddaughter Margaret Beaufort was the mother of Henry Tudor, the first Welsh king of Great Britain. The Tory Beauforts looked upon the Whig Morgan family as mere provincials and successfully blocked their initial attempts to elevate to the ranks of the aristocracy and it was not until 1859 that Sir Charles Morgan was created 1st Baron, Tredegar. The Beauforts' ownership of land locally led to leases for the construction of the Union Ironworks at The Garn, Rhymney Bridge, for limestone quarrying at Trefil and for the construction of a branch tramroad line from Nantybwch to the Union Works.

5. One of the holdings of the Beaufort Estate was Nant-y-Gaseg Farm, one of the older farms of the area that was situated in a dip beyond the Graig Chapel at Rhymney Bridge. Once the abode of the Thomas family, its situation on 'Blayne Rompeney' (Blaen Rhymney) provided the summer grazing for what was basically a sheep farm. Older farms, nevertheless, made themselves as self-sufficient as possible and would grow whatever crops and vegetables they could as well as keeping milking cows for the production of milk, cheese and butter.

Wooden butter print

6. An example of traditional butter churning on a farm which produced its own butter and cheese. The secret of good butter making was to ensure that every particle of water was squeezed out in its preparation. This would have been undertaken with large, specially crafted spoons, which were often designed with a distinctive pattern, were greatly treasured and were handed down from mother to daughter. It has been said that Welsh spoons have their origin in the butter spoon which traditionally had a similar web pattern.

9

7.   Domestic activities in older farms and cottages have always traditionally been associated with the hearth, or aelwyd, especially during the winter months. The hearth symbolised both a focus ('focus' - Latin for 'fireplace') on the home and on the converging point for family activities. The vast majority of cottages had a single hearth, especially after the imposition of the Hearth Tax in the 17th century, and only the lesser gentry and above were able to afford the luxury of having two or more fireplaces in their homes. Early hearths were simply large open grates fuelled with peat, wood, furze, gorse or straw on which everything was cooked but, later, stone ovens were constructed alongside the fire in which baking could be undertaken. In many farmhouses the fires were kept burning continuously for decades and to let them go out was to invite bad luck. The task of covering and uncovering the fire every evening and morning was taken very seriously.

8.   The association of the hearth with the family, its continuity and 'belonging' persisted for many centuries with the daily process of 'dadanudd', the uncovering of the ashes each morning to allow the fire to come to life. So important was the concept that it even appeared in ancient Welsh laws in association with the possession rights of a man and his home. The tradition of the squatter's cottage or 'Ty Unnos', built hastily overnight, was not complete, and ownership was not secured, until a fire had been lit and smoke was seen to rise from the chimney by the morning. This law traces itself back to the days of the Silurian tribal communities when a man entitled himself to a parcel of land if, between the hours of sunset and sunrise, he was able to build a house, complete with roof, upon it. The amount of land surrounding his house to which he became entitled depended on how far he was able to throw an axe from the four corners of the construction. Centuries ago this system for acquiring a home and land was widespread, and easily achieved, especially as help could be enlisted in gathering stones in advance and with the actual construction. The photograph above shows an example of what a Ty Unnos looked like with its turf roof and quickly built shell. My thanks are extended to the St. Fagans Museum of Welsh Life for kindly allowing its reproduction.

Such constructions were widespread locally, particularly on the Dowlais Common, when workers coming into the area in the 18th century to work in the blast furnaces took advantage of this ancient law to supply themselves with rent-free homes. The Marquess of Bute and the Duke of Beaufort, who owned the land, were at first tolerant to the ever-increasing groups of cottages that were springing up and even allowed a certain flexibility with the building time. Their tolerance was challenged, however when cottagers began to take further land for their own purposes, for use as gardens and paddocks or on which to graze sheep and cattle. This serious, unauthorised encroachment on to their land and the steady build up of a mostly Irish community made it necessary for the land-owners, through their agents, to come down on the offenders and to take legal action to evict them from their properties.

9. This exquisite photograph of Blaen Rhymney Fach Farm, with its thatched roof, shows the abode of members of the Morgan family when taken at the turn of the century. Of historical importance its tenants, over the centuries, would have needed the many pastoral and domestic skills required to sustain their existence on the bare upland beyond Rhymney. A working knowledge of spinning and weaving was necessary, as was the making of dairy products, baking and smoking foods. Some farms would have contained a smithy, undertaken candle-making and woodworking as well as caring for their stock which would have included sheep, cattle, pigs and fowl. Pigeons were domesticated for the table and for their eggs. Everyone worked hard and each member of the family, however young, had a share in the duties.

10. Another of the older farm houses on the higher land above Rhymney is Pentwyn Farm which was built above the original valley forest-line and in easy reach of upland grazing. Such farms were a progression from the old seasonal system of migration when permanent settlements were in the low-lying sheltered 'hendre' but summer grazing was undertaken on the 'hafod', the upland summer pasture where shacks or huts would be occupied by shepherds throughout the summer months.

11. A washing paddle and smoothing iron which were two of the many domestic implements used in kitchens. The paddle or dolly would have been used by the washer woman to squeeze dirt from clothing as she twisted and turned them in hot water. The implement was made of sycamore by the local wood-turner. Washing additives included fuller's earth, chalk and clay to remove grease. Onion juice, lemon juice and urine were used to remove certain stains with milk being included to combat acidic stains such as vinegar, urine and fruit juices. Flannel was often cleaned with a soap made from specially prepared balls of fern. The smoothing or box iron, patented in Germany by Dalli, was widely made and used elsewhere and was heated by a compacted charcoal. It featured a row of holes on each side for ventilation purposes.

12. This photograph of an old-type baking oven shows the large wooden spade or 'peel' that was used to take the bread from the oven. Everyone did their own bread-baking, usually weekly, either individually or in communal ovens which were situated either indoors or outside. Outside ovens, commonly used in this part of Wales, were generally dome-shaped and made of clay. Indoor ovens were heated separately to the main fire and the ashes removed before baking took place. On days when baking was not undertaken cakes could be cooked on a bakestone or griddle directly over the fire. Ashes were removed or spread out in the oven prior to baking by a rake or 'corlac'.

13. Looking north to Rhymney Bridge at the confluence of the three counties of Glamorgan, Monmouthshire and Breconshire, an area important also because it historically contains the boundaries of the Beaufort, Bute and Morgan (Tredegar) estates. So important has boundary recognition been to estate owners over the centuries that it was necessary for them and their tenants to 'beat the boundaries' by physically walking them each year. This proved to be an exciting event for villagers when, on the day, all work would be abandoned and, headed by the Parish Clerk or Estate Bailiff, they would proceed to walk the boundaries of their holdings following certain well-practised rituals on the way. Through pond, stream or bog they would follow their well-trodden path, guided by trees and piles of stones that had been sited there centuries before. At certain points along the route the Clerk and the Bailiff, armed with sticks, would seize hold of a small boy and administer several smart strokes across his back at the same time as reciting the words 'Remember the Parish boundary line'. The young lads did not mind this too much as their inducement was a good feast gratefully received at the expense of the Parish. Another event on the Beaufort estate which caused considerable excitement was the grouse shoot which took place twice each year at August and towards Christmas. The Duke's tenants, who acted as beaters, would meet at Trefil and comb the moor, driving the birds towards the waiting gentry. Their reward was a packed picnic lunch which they ate with gusto at the Duke's Table, Trefil, washed down with liberal quantities of ale. The above photograph shows the area known as The Garn where was constructed Rhymney's first ironworks, The Union, built in 1801 by a group of Bristol industrialists.

14. Situated to the south of Rhymney House, all that now remains of the Union Blast Furnace is a pile of stones.

15. A view down Graig Row, Rhymney Bridge, which was built at the turn of the 19th century to house ironworkers in the Union Works below. It was a two-tiered development built into the embankment with upper and lower dwellings and provided homes for sixteen families. The single storey upper level shown led directly on to the pathway, had stable-type doors, small windows, attics with tiny windows in the tiled roof and no back access. Below, to the rear, the dwellings of Lower Graig Row consisted of two small rooms with, again, a stable door and two small windows. They also had a small back room underground built into the embankment. Mrs. Morris lived at number three Upper Graig Row and sold home-made sweets from her pantry which included toffee made from coarse dark sugar, boiled sweets, mints, ribbon liquorice, Spanish root, malt balls and toffee apples. Elizabeth Price was born in nearby Graig House in the 1890s and reminisced fondly on her place of birth when interviewed by the author in 1984. She remembered colliers wearing white 'duck' trousers which were made by their wives, rough, cream-coloured waistcoats and striped white flannel shirts. Sunday best shirts were embroidered in white cotton down their fronts. Underwear, again flannel, was a one-piece item of clothing called a 'drover' which went from neck to knee. She recalled socks being knitted with four pins and how important red flannel was to wear, particularly to cover the chest to prevent worsening of an illness. Older ladies wore black bonnets and capes. Mrs Price remembered a toll-house and toll-gate on Rhymney Bridge, where the bus shelter now stands, with a large gate across the road through which carriages could not pass without first paying the required toll fee. Her grandfather was the sexton at Graig cemetery and she recollected a lady of Lower Graig Row who made pop from nettles and rhubarb, boiled with sugar and yeast and of pork from a freshly killed pig being salted and put outside on the 'vainc' for a fortnight before being hung up in the rafters to dry. Her amazing memory provided a vivid picture and intriguing insight into the way of life of her early childhood.

16. Graig House, shown above, where Elizabeth Price lived, was situated in the dip between Rhymney Bridge and Graig Chapel. It has also served as the residence of previous ministers.

17. This charming photograph of The Windsor Arms, Collins Row, Butetown, was taken in 1878 when Rees Harris, shown at its door, was 'mine host' at a time when quoit-throwing , played with horse-shoes, proved to be a particularly popular pastime. His grandson, also called Rees Harris, continues to live in Collins Row.

18. A later social activity in Butetown was amateur dramatics and here we see the Cwmnu Dramadol, Drenewydd in 1928, the cast of which were on this occasion performing their presentation of 'Y Ffon Dafe'. Standing from left to right are to be seen Will Bassett, Jim Howells, Rebecca Breeze, Gwyneira Jenkins, Lena Bassett, Jim Oakley and John Pugh. Seated are May Jenkins (nee Jones), Tom Edwards, a young Eddie Mumford, Tommy Jones (the shop) and Nancy Jones who lived at Halfway House, near Pantywaun. This particular group took second prize in a popular Rhondda Valley competition that year.

19. Rhymney House, built in 1801 as the residence of the Manager of the Union Blast Furnace, near Rhymney Bridge, was designated as a listed building of Special Architectural and Historic Interest in 1971. For many years the home of the Maddox family, the ground was leased by them from the Duke of Beaufort (as a Breconshire holding) in 1902 for an annual rent of £20. Grand in its appearance and dimensions it was approached by a carriageway drive and contained in its ground floor dining, drawing and breakfast rooms, kitchen, school-room and offices. The first floor contained four large bedrooms and a bathroom/water-closet. Outside were the coach-house and substantial stables, together with a large kitchen garden and ornamental grounds.

20. This fascinating 1936 wedding photograph from the Maddocks (originally 'Maddox') family archive was taken in the grounds of Rhymney House. The bride is the sister of Freddie Maddocks, a well-known butcher who traded on the High Street in Rhymney. On the extreme right can be seen Morgan Gronow who taught in the Upper Rhymney Primary School, then in Cambrian Street.

21. This old photograph of Red House Row (named from nearby Ty Coch Farm) and Carno Pit Row before redevelopments had taken place, will surely evoke nostalgia in older residents who remember the area. Built, similarly to Upper Cross Row, as back to back houses with one room up and one down, some families broke through the dividing wall to double the size of their living quarters. The homes of such families as the Rists, Pughs, Browns, Muttons and Robertsons, the cottages had their fair share of well-known personalities. There was Ike Moseley who kept pigs in the nearby allotment, Dai Sando, the very tall 'Long Annie' who always dressed in black and one-legged pigeon fancier Billy Burch. Tim Patch, who lived by Becca's sweet shop, enjoyed working his allotment and Sid Brown's wife, Mabel, made mouth-watering faggots and peas which she sold to neighbours, often being paid, instead, with a bucket of coal. The Robertsons made toffee and another family made small beer from nettles and barm bought from the brewery.

22. Tim Patch, mentioned above, fully named Timothy Davies, lived from 1870 to 1954 and was well known for the support and advice he gave on legal matters to the poor people of the area. Literate, widely read and self-taught he became a mines' official and a force to be reckoned with in local political and social affairs. A Methodist and a member of nearby Ebenezer Chapel he became particularly expert in the Poor Law which he put to good use in his advice on social security matters and with students' grant applications. A miner who received his nickname from the 'patches', local areas where coal and ironstone were prolifically mined, he stood out from his contemporaries with such eccentric touches as when he used the skin of his dead cat as a cover for his bible, its tail serving as a page marker. Tim Patch lived in number 13 Carno Pit Row and enjoyed further success with his literary ability in taking joint first prize in the 1901 Gwent Chair Eisteddfod with John Edwards of 58 High Street, Rhymney for their essays on the history of Rhymney. Tim Patch was a great friend of Aneurin Bevan who was best man at his wedding.

23.   The Clarence Inn was built in the early 1800s and witnessed the many trials and tribulations that the Old Rhymney experienced in her tough upbringing. Hotels and inns were focal points for a wide range of activities, one of which was as a meeting place for benevolent societies. The Clarence in its earlier years played host to the Philanthropic Order of True Ivorites which was a Welsh language order founded in 1836 whose President and Grand Master at the time was Brother Enoch James and its secretary Thomas Thomas. Their worthy host at the Clarence Inn was Councillor Benjamin Rees who was manager of the inn for 23 years. Rees came to Rhymney from Llanelly in the 1850s to work for Andrew Buchan at the Rhymney Company Shop and then as a brewery clerk. He became manager of the Clarence in 1881 but met an untimely end in 1904 when, in unusual circumstances, he drowned in 21 inches of water in a well in the cellar of the inn when fetching beer. The well, 2 feet 4 inches square and 2 feet deep, was protected by a frame and wooden cover yet Rees, mysteriously, was found dead, head and shoulders in the water.

24.   Public houses were also a centre for competitive events such as horseshoe-pitching, shove ha'penny, feats of strength, barefist fighting and places such as the Rhymney Inn had their own cock-fighting pits. The inn's personalised tokens were often paid out as prizes to winners which ensured that the winnings were returned to behind the bar. Above we see a 3d token that was issued by the Clarence Inn, believed to have been used as prizes for skittle tournaments and which could be exchanged for beer.

25. The area of Carno became a crossroads of activity when the early industrialisation of nearby Dowlais demanded more and more iron ore and coal for its furnaces. Materials mined at Ras Bryn Oer and elsewhere were brought by mule and pack-horse to the river ford at Carno for sale and collection by the ironmasters' agents until the construction of local iron furnaces began in the early 19th century. The Carno area was then soon to become otherwise engaged in clay-mining and brick-making with a clay mine at Clarendon Row being managed for 41 years by surveyor and chief shotsman Enoch James. James was a competent surveyor who, with considerable skill, produced charts from his subterranean surveying of pits, drifts, airways, headings and faces of the considerable workings that lay beneath Rhymney. He left Rhymney to live in California in 1890. With a labyrinth of almost a hundred clay, coal and iron-ore mines in and around Rhymney it was inevitable that cave-ins and subsequent subsidences would often occur and, it has not been unknown for whole kitchens (in Harcourt Street) and gardens (Gladstone Terrace) to vanish below ground. Our photograph above shows the remains, right of centre, of the brickworks which was situated between the road and the railway line.

26. Carno Houses were built behind where Glan Elyrch now stands and were of back-to-back construction, having been some of the oldest cottages of the village. It was one of the earliest communities in industrial Rhymney and built over coal-level workings from which the inhabitants continuously heard the movement of trams and mining activity below.

27. Workmens' houses in ironmaking and coal-mining communities were generally of three types, each in keeping with the occupational status of the tenants for whom they were built. The best, earlier-built houses, such as Brewery Row, White Row and Tre-Edwards shown above, had two storeys, four small sash windows, a fairly roomy kitchen and side room at floor level and a large and small bedroom upstairs. The best class of workmen usually lived here and, for the most part, kept their houses in an admirable state of cleanliness and order. Stone floors were sanded, coloured or patterned, showy dressers displayed china and glassware and solid chairs and tables would be highly polished. Kitchen ceilings were not plastered and the rafters were used for hanging up crockery or other kitchen implements. Second-class houses had generally two rooms, one above stairs and one below and third-class cottages might have only one room where the poorest class of labourer might live with his family.

28. Seen throughout Rhymney, this was the typical scenario of a miner's cottage when he returned home at the end of his shift and will be vividly remembered by older readers. Working clothes needed to be dried for the following day's shift and this was accomplished by draping them around the open coal fire which glowed intensely throughout the day. The miner himself, and his father and sons if necessary, bathed naked in a large tub on the hearth. The cast-iron fire-place had ovens either side for cooking and bread-making and a bakestone (which was originally made of stone, but later iron) would be used on the fire for making Welshcakes and scones.

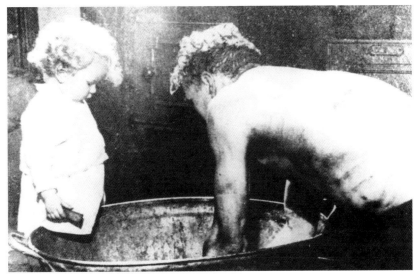

29. Bath-time was a protracted and often ritualistic affair in some households when as many as eight or more miners would return home from their shift. The senior member of the household usually bathed first and, on his knees, would wash his upper torso, face and head. He would then sit in the bath and wash his lower half. The back would sometimes remain unwashed in the superstitious belief that it prevented the miner from catching a cold. The most junior of the family went last by which time the water was invariably as black as he. Younger members of the family, exhausted from a hard day in the pit, often fell asleep on the floor, in which case they would be gently rolled under the table until it was their time to wash. The mother of the family, assisted by her daughters, had the responsibility for boiling buckets of water on the fire in readiness for their arrival from work. Bathing was conducted in front of the family in often one room cottages and visiting neighbours were not in the slight deterred by this necessary daily event. The bathwater, when finished with, would be emptied out through the back door.

Tubs were originally made of wood by coopers and resembled barrels cut in half. They were later superseded by zinc baths which were lighter and which could be hung on a wall peg in the back yard. Following a bath the collier's eyes looked as if they had received an application of mascara because of the residual coal-dust that adhered to the eyelashes. This would be cleaned away with vaseline. Blue scars were also a trademark of the collier and they could sometimes be alleviated by honey if applied at an early stage. Possibly, because of the properties of the coal dust, such cuts rarely seemed to become infected.

30. A group of miners, among whom are to be seen Dick Pugh, B. Watkins, Morgan Rees, Bill Rees and D. Lance, who would have experienced colliery life before the luxury of pithead baths.

31. Accidents, infection and disease were major hazards in the Old Rhymney and the cholera epidemic which swept through the town in 1849, and the many deaths that it caused, was a reflection of the poor living conditions that existed at that time. Infectious diseases had to be controlled and isolation hospitals were built behind Ramsden Street (then Pit Row), at Hospital Houses near the brewery and in Jerusalem Street (then known as Dockers Row). A familiar sight in much later years was the first mentioned, situated in the Cutting and later to become the home of the Howells family. This was an isolation hospital, with its associated morgue, from which patients could be transferred to Cardiff Infirmary.

32. Before and around the early 1800s ironmasters cared little for the welfare of their workforce and ironstone and coal miners, if injured at work, were brought home on doors or planks of wood and deposited, often dying, on their doorsteps. It was not unknown for their workmates who carried them home to be docked part of their wages for the time they lost. The setting up of sick funds, sometimes paid for by deductions from wages, brought later improvements and relief payments during sickness, old age and to meet burial expenses came into being. The Rhymney Workmans Medical Aid Fund was established in 1878. The above photograph shows a hand-cart that was used in the coal industry to transport stretcher cases.

33. The Terrace was constructed in the 1820s as superior living accommodation for the higher echelons of the Rhymney iron industry. A large imposing detached house was built at either end of the terrace to house the Manager of the Company Shop and the Chief Colliery Manager. Next to these came two intermediate-sized houses for the Company Shop cashier and the assistant general manager. In between were built smaller houses for lesser managers, surgeons, the Company police officer and chief foremen. A rise in status in the industry generally meant a move right or left into larger accommodation and while living in the smaller middle houses one never 'took tea' in either of the the end homes. End families were 'church' and central families 'chapel' which in itself formed an effective social barrier. A tramroad ran directly in front of The Terrace (originally called Buchan's Terrace) on which ironstone, coal and timber were continuously hauled by horse and later by steam engine to the iron furnaces and pits.

34. Price Street was the home of the nationally renowned poet Ioan Gwent (John Watkins, 1843-1889) who came to Rhymney with his father from Carno in Montgomeryshire to work as a young miner. Following an accident underground in which he broke his leg he was introduced to poetry by his father during his convalescence. The poetry he read he digested voraciously and his development as a poet was fired with enthusiasm. His first successful eisteddfod poem was 'Y Gwlithyn' (The Dewdrop) for which he won a Chair in Cardiganshire in 1876. His Chair was exhibited in Price Street until the early 1900s by his family. Further success was achieved when a small volume of his poetry was published in 1880 called 'Tlysau Awen' (Treasures of the Muse).

35. Rhymney's first Constitutional Club was housed in Mount Pleasant in a building that had originally been the base of the Salvation Army. Reportedly haunted by a lady in grey costume and bonnet, it was said that she was a returning Salvation Army member unable to rest because of the ungodly levels of drinking and revelry that were taking place in her once haven of prayer.

36. The above twist box belonged to Edwin Thomas who lived in Forge Street and Pontlottyn. He was a local carpenter who also made objects of interest and functional use from brass. Such containers, now collectors' pieces, were once the prized possessions of miners who filled them with twist tobacco which they chewed underground to collect inhaled coal-dust particles, then to be spat out. The boxes often exhibited a high degree of individuality and craftsmanship in which their owners took great pride. They were sometimes made in the colliery lamproom during quiet spells or bought as blanks for personal ornamentation. Coming in various shapes and sizes they invariably served as a means of personal identification for the owner or for the job that he was doing. Christmas Davies of Lower Ras Bryn Oer Farm, who also owned and worked his own coal level, had the words 'Bogey Man' engraved on his twist box, indicating the underground drams or 'bogies' on which he worked.

37. The rear aspect of Forge Street and Cwm Shon Matthew Square with Brynhyfryd Chapel in the background. This area was colonized in the early 1800s, together with The Rock, Pontlottyn, by Irish immigrants fleeing the famine and poverty back home and seeking a living in the iron industry. The harsh conditions that they encountered, both at work and in their living conditions, brought an air of notoriety to the area and drunkeness, fighting and unrest were everyday eventualities. The mission of Father Theobald Mathew of Cork in 1838 excited much interest in those who sought a more temperate existence and under his influence the consumption of liquor became greatly reduced. Branches of the Rechabite Society later sprung up in Rhymney and the teetotal movement further greatly influenced the move of the many of the Irish contingency towards becoming champions of the pledge.

38. In Forge Street, opposite Moriah Street, was situated the Cyclops Inn, an old public house which was later to become a private dwelling. Its proprietor in 1852 was a certain Henry Jones and in 1862 William Scott. Inns were often named from occupations in the iron industry, and frequented by workers in those occupations and the Cyclops Inn would likely have received its name from the shinglers who worked at the Middle and Lower Union furnaces nearby. Shinglers were men who hammered the hot iron after it had been puddled and were susceptible to the continuous rain of iron sparks which were thrown off. To protect them, a specialised leather dress which covered all the body was worn, reinforced with large metal plates. On their feet they wore heavy boots which were sturdy enough to be handed down from father to son. Their heads were covered with a leather hood in the centre of which was a single large glass eye through which they viewed their work. The complete assembly was an awesome sight and earned the shinglers the nickname 'Cyclops' for obvious reasons. The Cyclops Inn, like the Puddlers Arms, was reminiscent of the tough workers who toiled in those hot and dangerous conditions and who needed a place of social refuge in which to quaff their huge thirsts.

CHAPTER 2

Trade and Industry

Before 1800 the Rhymney area was completely rural save for the comparatively small amount of mining that took place to satisfy the needs of smithies and later the Dowlais iron furnaces. It was not until 1802 when the Union furnace was built that a true industrial revolution began in the area. Up until then the indigent locals had for centuries made their living from the land, growing crops, from sheep and cattle farming and through trading their cottage produce at markets and fairs. Cottage industries were widespread and a surprising wealth of activities took place to help sustain a living. Of local importance, in an area such as Llechryd where sheep farming was widely undertaken, would be wool-spinning and hand-loom weaving and farms that could afford them would utilise spinning wheels within their households, often operated by their servants.   Other crafts pursued would be wood-carving, clog-making, rush-plaiting, candle-making, butter and cheese making and the making of a variety of confectionery.

The onset of industrialization in Rhymney, with a quickly increasing population and numbers of retail outlets on the streets, in some respects brought benefits to the indigenous cottagers. A ready market became available for selling crops through the Company Shops, the demand for meat dramatically increased and farmhorses were contracted for the haulage of ores and general goods. A further change was the transition from cottage industries to wholesale production of goods and every hamlet had its own woollen mill where sheep farmers would take their wool to be cleansed, spun and woven or where wool, already spun and weaved at home, would be taken for making up into cloth and blankets. Mills were initially situated on river banks and powered by water-wheel then later by steam. They are recorded at such places as Bargoed, Brithdir and Gelligaer but areas such as Carno and Nant y Melyn lent themselves quite favourably to this kind of widespread activity. The arrival of the iron industry, and the huge population increase that it brought, meant that beef on the hoof had to be brought in to stock the Company Shops and farms such as Pwll y Glo, with their own corn mills and saddlery, were used to store and slaughter the cattle brought in by drovers.

As the iron industry grew so home industries dwindled and the small smithy at Rhymney Bridge, the shoemaker in his cottage and the maidservant using her spinning spindle on an isolated cottage on Rhymney Hill became redundant or were drawn into the new developments.

39.   The dramatic transition from rural Rhymney to industrial Rhymney is beautifully depicted in the above painting of the Rhymney Ironworks in the early 1800s, undertaken by Penry Williams.

40. Woollen manufacture has been practiced for thousands of years by farmers who would take wool from their own flocks and with simple equipment produce the yarns, blankets, cloth and flannels that they required for their everyday use. The stretching of the raw wool, carding, was first of all undertaken with the use of teasels and spinning done on hand-held spindles and whorls. In the 14th century was invented the 'great walking wheel' which was turned by hand and this was used until the 17th century when the innovative foot treadle was invented. Shown aside is a photograph of the 'great walking wheel' tended by a young Miss Blodwen Price, suitably dressed in the costume of the day, and taken in 1900. The spinning wheel was an essential part of the furnishings of many cottages, farms and country homes and its competent use was an essential qualification for the women of the house, including its servants. The word 'spinster' relates to the process of spinning and, unlike weaving, was never carried out by men. Later came the hand-powered spinning jenny, too large for cottages and requiring a special building, to be followed by the spinning mule or jack, larger again and powered by a water-wheel.

41. Coarse cloth, or 'brychan', was weaved from the spun wool as a domestic craft on small looms and often undertaken by men. Some farmers, in addition to tending their cattle and sheep, would keep a small loom in an outbuilding and produce the yarn they required for their families or for sale. Others might take their wool to a weaver when no money would exchange hands but, instead, the weaver would keep back some of the wool, often a tenth, as payment.

42. Place names such as 'Pandy', 'Melyn Bach', and, sometimes 'Pant' indicate the location of fulling mills. Fulling was the process of shrinking, thickening and cleaning the newly woven cloth and then stretching it on a frame. In early times this would have been undertaken simply by placing the cloth in a stream and 'walking' upon it for hours and fulling mills retained the name 'Walk Mills' for many years. The photograph aside, taken from a carving on a gravestone, illustrates the Roman method of fulling with the fuller standing in a tub of warm, soft water trampling the cloth underfoot. The continual friction causes the wet woollen fibres to mat together, or 'felt', reducing the size of a piece of cloth by as much as a third. Fullers earth, soda or even human urine were first applied to the cloth to assist in the cleaning process. The 'walking' of cloth continued in the remoter parts of Wales until the early twentieth century before mechanisation took over.

43. The woollen shawl that was widely produced in Wales is shown wrapping the child securely, held in one arm and leaving the other arm free for other tasks. Red flannel was particularly favoured in South Wales, not only for its warmth, but for its supposed medicinal qualities. Red flannel smeared in goose-grease was seen as a cure for throat and chest infections and it was also widely worn by ironworkers as underwear to guard against rheumatism. In a sick room the bed and windows were covered with red flannel blankets, the walls painted red and visitors were required to wear red clothing in the belief that it helped to ward off illness. The belief continued until as recently as 1940 when Rhymney families were known to drape red curtains over the bedroom door of a child suffering from scarlet fever. Narrow strips of red cloth worn around the neck helped ward off whooping cough and the 'brick-girls' who worked in the brickyard near Clarendon Row all wore white-spotted red scarves around their necks. Such was the traditional belief in the colour red that a skein of scarlet-coloured silk tied around the neck, with exactly nine knots hanging at the front, was a sure prevention from nose-bleed.

44. In their early days the Company Shops of the Andrew Buchan empire completely monopolised retailing in Rhymney with the penurious truck system ensuring that workers were tied to the 'shop' and unable to buy their goods elsewhere. The eventual easing of their grip saw the growth of small shops and stores throughout the town and High Street became a centre of activity for trading in a wide variety of commodities. The turn of the century saw John Curtis trading as a fishmonger, boot and shoemaker and furniture dealer there; Tobias Fine was the pawnbroker and John Jenkin Jacobs the printer. Elizabeth Protheroe was an ironmonger, Thomas Griffiths the baker and John Howells the butcher. In number 99 lived cobbler and deacon Evan Davies whose son was to become the bardic poet 'Ossian Gwent', a patternmaker and further deacon. Mrs. Evans 'Llwyni' lived at number 98 from where she sold Welsh flannel. At 96 lived the Reverend T. E. Edwards, a steelworker turned preacher and in 95 the musical family of Eos Mynwy, the bardic 'Nightingale of Monmouthshire'.

45. 97 High Street was the home of cobbler Twynog Jeffries, the poet and writer, who traded there until 1911. In earlier Rhymney clogs were the common form of footwear for workers on the farm and in the ironworks, brickworks and mines and leather-soled footwear was the reserve of the better-off classes, being both expensive and difficult to obtain. Bare feet were commonplace and shoes or boots that were possessed were often used on special occasions only, such as when attending chapel. Clogs were usually made from the wood of the alder which grew on the river banks and which was preferred for its waterproof qualities, its softness and ease of carving. They were often made by itinerant clog-makers who would set up camp in an area, axe suitable trees and cut their boles into four different block sizes for men's, women's, children's and small children's clogs. The blocks were then shaped with an axe and carved with a specialised clogger's knife. Furnace workers, farmers, clay-miners, brickworkers and drift-mine workers all took advantage of this sturdy form of footwear which was often strengthened with metal strips and heavy nails.

46. Behind Forge Street was situated the Old Middle Furnace which joined, soon after its construction, with the Upper Furnace in Rhymney Bridge to become the Union Iron Works Company, a consortium of Richard Crawshay, Benjamin Hall, Richard Cunningham and Thomas Williams. The 'Rumney Estate' of the Ironworks was later, in 1824, bought by stock company Forman & Co. at about the same time that the neighbouring Bute Ironworks was being built. Forman was an extremely rich speculator with a lucrative position as an officer in the Tower of London and earned the nickname 'Billy Ready Money'. In 1837 the Union Works joined the Bute Works to become the Rhymney Iron Company with capital assets of £500,000. The Lord Mayor of London, the Right Honourable William Taylor Copeland, MP, became its chairman and, in 1843, he donated the silver chalices to St. David's Church.

47. Complementing the ironworks were the tramroads which carried mule and horse-drawn trams of coal and ironstone to the furnaces. The above photograph, showing a once familiar sight, highlights part of the original route of the tramway from Ras Bryn Oer to the Middle Furnace. Tram roadways were soon to network throughout Rhymney, threading through narrow streets and alongside cottages, fetching iron ore, clay, bricks, coal, stone and timber to wherever they were needed. This first tramway through Rhymney picked up its materials from the drift-mines on The Ras and proceeded down past the front of the cottages of Susannah Row. From here it went behind the now demolished houses of Upper and Lower Cross Row, crossed over the main street above Albion Square and proceeded down the middle of Price Street. It then went behind St. David's Church, behind Tan-y-Llan and the Eisteddfod Field dropping to the back of The Terrace and on to the tunnel under Surgery Hill shown above, eventually ending up at the Middle Furnace behind Forge Street. Mr. Hubbuch, the manager of the ironworks at the time, was responsible for the construction of the tunnel which goes below the grounds of the, now, Welsh School, originally the home of the manager himself. The imposing Rhymney Workmen's Institute can be seen behind.

48. This photograph shows the other end of Hubbuch's tunnel, the tramroad from which went on to the Middle Furnace below. Hubbuch was also responsible for the construction of the tramway which came from the Waun Pits behind the Memorial Park, past the old Co-operative Shop building and Havards Row, then dropping down through The Cutting behind Beulah Row. Over the years many miles of rail track was laid in the town, both above ground and below in mines and pits and in the age of steam loudly puffing engines were to be seen hauling trucks of goods from the brewery, past the front of The Terrace and Cottage Hospital, down to the Company Shop.

49. The age of the tramroads gave birth to the larger-gauge railway network which quickly developed in the middle of the 19th century. Horsepower gave way to steam and the days of the Rhymney Tramroad Company line to Newport were numbered when the wider gauge link to Cardiff Docks was made in 1858. The Rhymney Tramroad opened in 1836, at first carried horse-drawn trams to Newport, and the journey over the 22 miles took ten hours or more. The introduction of steam power in the early 1840s, because of the speed restrictions that were imposed, merely halved the time of the journey and this was not found to be satisfactory. The new railways were, on the other hand, vastly quicker and cheaper and soon large numbers of coal trucks and steel wagons were to be seen leaving Rhymney for Cardiff Docks.

31

50. Pidwellt Pit, entered through the Barracks Level, was situated opposite the brewery on the other side of the Rhymney River. It was sunk in 1856 and worked the Red, Blue and Rosser ironstone seams, then the Four Foot and Yard coal seams at a depth of 337 feet. The workings were later absorbed into the Pidwellt Colliery and in 1953 the old shaft was filled in.

51. A typical scenario at pit bottom in the days when a wooden cage carried four men to the pit floor. The dangerous environment carried many hazards, none more so than the risks of gas explosions. Firedamp was produced by vegetable matter that had decayed over thousands of years, the gas of which had become trapped in pockets underground. It was colourless, odourless and highly explosive when mixed with air and was detected by a blue flame on the lamp. Choke damp was a mixture of carbon dioxide and nitrogen and had the effect of putting out a flame because of oxygen starvation. In early mines an immediate escape from this gas was to lie on the stomach with the mouth as low to the floor as possible, preferably in a hole. If inhaled it was important to induce vomiting and the early miner might do this by filling his stomach with ale. A vital part of the fireman's job was to enter the mine first, to seek out any gases that might have accumulated, and to disperse them.

52. The building of the railways, together with the roadways and canals, in itself was to create a major industry. One only has to look at such constructions as the Pontlottyn viaduct, the railway embankment from Rhymney railway station to Rhymney Bridge and the tunnels and bridges in the area to realise the huge challenges that faced engineers in the early 1800s. And, it must be remembered, all this was accomplished by hand without the benefit of today's earth-moving equipment. Those responsible were the 'navvies', an abbreviation of 'navigators', a huge army of tough workmen who, sometimes working with local labour, moved around the country following railroads and canals that were continuously under construction. The South Wales navvies, more often of Scottish, Irish and Welsh descent, armed with shovels, picks and packs of dynamite, lived where the line was being constructed, either sleeping rough or in specially constructed huts. A typical hut would sleep 20 men, two to a bed, which cost them $1\frac{1}{2}$ pence a night each. If they slept on the floor the cost would be a $\frac{1}{4}$ penny. At one end of the hut was situated a huge pot of continually boiling water in which each navvy would suspend his own piece of meat in a linen bag to be cooked. They both ate and drank well and a good navvy was capable of shifting 20 tons of earth a day for which he could be paid as much as 25 pence, a very good daily wage for a labourer, although he might have to wait as long as two months before he got paid. Wages were paid in local inns or in specially constructed ale-houses built by the construction company on site. The company would similarly provide a shop in the vicinity thereby ensuring that much of the wages they paid out would be recovered through the sale of their often over-priced goods. Pay day for the navvies was the day when the locals stayed at home and locked their doors because of the drunken disruption, fighting and general lawlessness that continued until they returned to work, perhaps days later. They worked hard, played hard and their death rate was high. Tunnels caved in or flooded and accidents occurred with careless use of explosives when they hurried. Time cost money to the contracting company and navvies could be easily replaced so little attention or sympathy was paid by them when injuries took place and a widow would be lucky to receive £5 compensation should her husband be killed. The era of the traditional navvy was slowly phased out with the introduction of steam power, and the workers who lived by their own laws, distinctively dressed in their moleskin trousers, canvas shirts, hob-nailed boots and gaudy red neckerchiefs were soon to become another piece of history.

The above photograph shows a representation of a navvy, tooled up, crossing the bridge at Carno. Beyond is part of the Rhymney River that was diverted by Andrew Buchan with his gangs of navvies and, on the right, the railway embankment that they built from Rhymney railway station to Rhymney Bridge.

53. Construction of the Rhymney railway line begun in 1854 and the station was built on the site of the Office School which was taken down and reconstructed as the Middle Rhymney School in 1857. Until then minerals and goods for export were being transported to Newport by the Tramroad Company on a line that ran through Abertysswg and New Tredegar. The opening of the speedier Rhymney Valley line in 1857, later to link with Bute Docks, was a day for celebration and immense crowds were to be seen at Rhymney station as the maiden transportation of heavily-laden trucks of iron was to take place. The 5th April, 1858, was another festive occasion when the first passenger train down the valley, gaily decorated with flags and bunting, was to leave full to the brim with laughing passengers in top hats and crinolines.

54. The Rhymney railway line was extended northwards in 1871 to join the existing London and North Western line through Nantybwch and a link station was built at Rhymney Bridge. In those early days signal boxes were lit by Tilley lamps, illuminated by gas mantles, and required constant pumping to maintain their pressure. Guards, porters and shunters carried hand lamps with red, green and clear windows and a sharp flick of the wrist was required to change colour. Nationalization in 1947 took the control of the railways out of private hands and into government control with the birth of British Railways. Above is the Rhymney Bridge station with a GWR train arriving from Cardiff. Inset are the stationmaster and three of his staff, one of whom is Oliver 'Ollie' Jones who lived in nearby Pen y rheol house. Although the station was bleak, almost 1,100 feet above sea level and at the end of a 1 in 35 single line gradient from Rhymney station, it, in its day, was a very busy junction for the Midlands and the North.

55.   From Scottish carpenter and farm worker at Abertysswg Farm to the manager of a navvy gang diverting the course of the Rhymney River was to develop a man of huge impact in the town and the driving force behind the success of the Rhymney brewing empire. Andrew Buchan was appointed manager of the Company Shop in 1836 and also manager of the Rhymney Iron Company's brewery when it came into business in 1839. The brewery was conceived because of the Company's realization that work in the heat of the furnaces gave men an abnormal thirst. In 1839 the chairman of the company, William Copeland, thereupon 'recommended the propriety of building a brewhouse for the supply of beer to all persons employed in the Works', and this was immediately put into effect.

56.   The brewery took on its manager's name and above we see the entrance to the brewery yard with the familiar Andrew Buchan clock at its portal. Buchan was an astute businessman but was also well remembered for his sympathetic and benevolent outlook, especially towards the children of the town. It was not unknown for him, on seeing a small boy with a ragged cap, to throw the cap over a hedge and take the boy to a local shop where he would be bought a new one, inevitably accompanied by a bag of biscuits. He was a prolific snuff taker, often to the distress of passing children into whose eyes it might have blown. A gift of a shilling more often than not quickly dried their tears. The brewery prospered for thirty years with Buchan at the helm and his passing away in 1870 caused considerable mourning in the valley.

57. Rhymney Brewery closed in April 1978 and all production was transferred to Cardiff. Before its buildings were pulled down the Andrew Buchan clock, which by now had been transferred to the wall of the coopers' shop, was again removed and fixed into the east-facing wall of the Old Company Shop at the bottom of Surgery Hill. Here we see Ron Moseley, brothers John and David 'Doc' Jones and Windsor Walters undertaking its removal watched by passer-by Elvet Dunn. The photograph was taken by ex-brewery employee Elvet Jones of the Ras Farm.

58. Synonymous with the brewery is the Rhymney Hobby Horse shown above. In 1920 control of the brewing passed from the Rhymney Iron Company into the hands of the Powell Duffryn Steam Coal Company but, in 1929, it became a company within its own right under the title Andrew Buchan Breweries Ltd. Its first chairman was Lt. Col. G L Hoare, C.B.E., who served the company for 23 years until his retirement in 1952. The hobby-horse trademark was adopted soon after his appointment and remained a formidable symbol until the brewery's closure. The man on the barrel was designed by a keen sportsman, one of the Pritchard brewing family of Crumlin, whose assets had been bought up by Buchans in 1930.

59. The longest serving employee of Rhymney Brewery Ltd was Sid Allen of nearby White Row who retired in 1963 after 56 years with the company. His service, as deliveryman to the company's South Wales public houses, spanned the days of dray-horses and steam and petrol-driven lorries. Sid is seen above receiving his long-service award, a gold watch, from company chairman Col. Harry Llewellyn, C.B.E., J.P., at the Rhymney Breweries canteen in Cardiff, where a total of 141 employees received their awards. Amazingly, Sid remained teetotal throughout his life.

60. Sid Allen again, on this occasion in June 1935 standing besides one of the many vehicles with which he was to become familiar, the old petrol No. 5. The photograph was taken on the brewery forecourt which, you will notice, was then uncobbled. Sid would have experienced the changes in ownership of the brewery and its expansion with the acquisition of Crosswells, Cardiff, the Taff Vale Brewery at Merthyr, its association with Whitbreads and its amalgamation with the Llanfoist Brewery.

61. Workers' welfare was always an important consideration at Rhymney Brewery and it had its own sports club to which both employer and employee contributed and in which members elected their own officers. The above is the first committee of the Rhymney Brewery Sports Club which opened its clubhouse alongside Clarendon Row in the 1950s. The Committee consisted of, from top left, Davies the Chemist, Glyn 'The Baron' Davies, Bill Pullman, David Morgan, John Williams 'Coker', unknown, John Newell and, I am afraid, unknown. Seated are Jackie Woods, John Davies, D R Cox, Eirwen Morgan, John Henry Thomas and Ken Newell.

62. 1974 saw the conversion of the Drill Hall next to The Terrace into the new Brewery Club with all the additional room, facilities and provisions that it brought. Social activities increased and here we see its manager David Jones and wife Lena being presented with a 'wish you well' token by Ann of the Ladies' Darts Team. Standing behind are to be seen Jacqueline Griffiths, Nelly Tovcoscvy, Annette Morgan and sister, Betty Newell and Nancy Ward.

63. Another dray lorry on a cold winter's day makes a delivery to the Royal Hotel, Rhymney. Petrol transportation brought a huge improvement in the area that could be covered for deliveries within one day. Earlier steam-driven vehicles when introduced were severely restricted by an 8 mph speed limit but even these allowed a wider range of activity to their predecessors, the drayhorses. The age of the drayhorse, which came to an end in Rhymney in the early 1900s, provided a rich experience for those employees fortunate enough to work with these fine animals. The huge Clydesdales and Shires, some a ton in weight, needed a powerful hand and special care was taken by the brewery to find handlers such as farmers and ploughmen who had sufficient strength and experience. Recruitment was mostly undertaken through such publications as 'The Hereford and Kidderminster Times' which was why Welshmen, employed in the ironworks and unaccustomed to handling such animals, were never seen in this work. Farmworkers jumped at the opportunity to take such work where they were paid the princely sum of 18/6d (about 93p) a week, and a gallon of beer a day. This was a vast improvement on farming where they might have to work from dawn until dusk bringing up a wife and perhaps four children on 9/- (45p) a week with a half-day holiday on Good Friday and Christmas Day each year. The brewery also provided a house for 8/- (40p) a month, deducted from pay, and a garden where crops could be grown for his family - an absolute fortune when compared to his previous existence. Clifford Griffiths of Hill Street, Rhymney, who worked for 51 years as transport engineer at Rhymney Brewery, treasured vivid collective memories of his and his father's experiences when working there. His father, Fred Griffiths, began work there in 1890 as a farrier, tending to 42 dray horses at a time when there were three shoeing smiths employed there. Each drayman had three horses which he groomed daily and a four-wheeled dray that carried 12 barrels giving a gross weight load of 3 tons. Two horses were side-by-side in the shafts and the third, the leader, fixed in front. Horses were well cared for, fed the best hay cut into chaff and mixed with dried beans, peas, nuts and oats. They each had their own straw-bedded stall with their names painted brightly above and each knew exactly which stall was his. Mr Griffiths recalls such names as Boxer, Duke, Tiger, Beauty, Lion, Sandy, Sailor, Mighty and Stingo. He also remembers the five or so cats that lived in the stables, each of which had its favourite horse on which to sleep, much to the apparent pleasure of its bed-mate. The drayhorses' working day was from 6 am to 6 pm during the week and from 6 am to 2 pm on Saturdays. Each had a wool-lined waterproof sheet in the dray to protect against the rain and heaven help the drayman should any return with a wet back. Their intelligence and homing instinct became legendary and on many a dark winter's night they could be seen bringing home a sleeping drayman through darkened streets and from as far away as neighbouring valley towns. The leader always seemed to know his way home and would occasionally stop, instinctively, for the team to rest for a few minutes before moving on.

Injured or ailing horses would be sent to the Company's farm below Pontlottyn or to the old vicarage field at Nantllesg to aid their recovery. As a farrier one of Mr Griffiths senior's jobs was to give medical attention to the drayhorses. He remembers amputating the leg of a small horse and replacing it with a wooden leg after which the horse became capable of undertaking light duties. He also had the unpleasant task of putting down severely injured horses, which usually brought tears to the eyes of their associated draymen.

64. This fine Shire belonged to Gwen Parfitt's father who hired it out to the brewery to undertake dray work. An important stopping point on his round was the Queen's Hotel where he would eagerly consume his regular bucket of beer before continuing on his journey. Greatly looked forward to in mid-summer was the grand parade of drayhorses when they would be groomed to perfection, their manes and tails plaited with coloured ribbons and fresh straw and their brasses and leathers highly polished. Drays would shine with polish and the draymen, adorned in top hats and cockades, would be finely turned out for competition. Prizes were presented for the best display by the Chairman of the Council. The onset of the First World War brought great sadness and gloom to the brewery. It was a time when both drayhorses and steam-driven lorries were in use and when large horses were being requisitioned by the government for the war effort. A government official is remembered calling at the brewery following which three strings of the finest horses were led to the railway station, loaded into horse-box vans and taken away. Their destination was France where they were to haul the big guns to the front line, never to be seen again. Few horses now remained at Rhymney, mostly the older ones, some of which were to end up pulling hearses in Rhymney and Pontlottyn. This was when mechanised transport of the brewery's products really came into its own.

Andrew Buchan

65. These were the service medals that were presented by Rhymney Brewery to its employees in recognitition of their loyal service. Mr. Clifford Griffiths' medals, following his 51 years with the company, are on display in Cardiff Museum.

66. Some male staff of James Smith & Co. (Derby) Ltd. enjoy their Christmas festivities in the 1970s. Among the happy smiling faces can be seen Dai Brown, Ron Griffiths, Vic Davies, Gwyn Williams, Dan Davies, Hadyn Jones, Eddie Collins, Tony Paxton, Cai Rowland and Freddie Tipping.

67. Another Christmas night out, this time the ladies of the brewery in 1965. From left to right, clearly having a great time in the Plymouth Arms, Pentrebach, Merthyr are Dwynwen Lyons, Rene (Matthews) Jones, Glenys Pritchard Davies, Doreen Price, Hilda Price, Olwen Jones, Margaret Jones, Gwyneth Williams, Esther (Doyle) Jones and Verena Harris.

68. When rows of houses were built in early Rhymney by the Rhymney Iron Company for its employees it was common practice for an end building, a lean-to, to be added to serve as a bakery where communal baking could be carried out. This usually simply consisted of an oven to which ready-mixed dough could be brought for baking. Such communal ovens were situated at Clarendon Row, Sun Row (Lower High Street), Plantation Street, Forge Street, Hill Street and Upper High Street and there were many others throughout the town. The Upper High Street bakery, shown above, on the right hand side of the buildings, originated in the 1850s and was a centre for local community baking where a penny would be charged for each loaf baked. Customers would make a secret mark on their dough for identification purposes and later collected their loaf of bread, baked, in a cloth basket. In earlier days such bakeries were often run by widows of men killed in the ironworks. Such women were usually destitute and were allowed to live on the bakehouse premises rent-free and given a free allocation of coal each week with which to run the oven. Customers were honour-bound to also give the widow a basin of flour which helped her eke out a living at a time when widows' compensation was unheard of. The above premises was later taken over as a business by Mary 'Bacus' Richards, the esteemed vocalist and conductor of the Rhymney Ladies Choir whose picture has been inserted. The corner shop shown was a cobblers owned by Dick Short of Bryn Seion Street, the father of Welsh schoolmistress Doris Short. To its right, in 1868, was the undertaking business of Thomas Jones Y Saer of Price Street which still exists today in the family name.

69. Another family of bakers, the Colliers, have baked bread in Rhymney for over 100 years. Their bakehouse in Goshen Street was established in 1873 and the photograph above shows the delivery cart which was used by the grandfather of the late Eli Collier. The bowler-hatted attendant, the aproned bakery hands and the horse-drawn carriage all help capture the essence of the time.

70. The India and China Tea Company on the High Street will be remembered by older people of Rhymney and here we see a young assistant, Miss Lucy (Coleman) Thomas, who worked there between the first and second world wars, on this occasion in the early 1920s. The well-stocked windows paint a different picture to that which existed during and following the war years when food was in desperately short supply. It was a time of ration books, identity cards, Spam and dried milk, when a packet of dried egg powder, equivalent to a dozen eggs, was distributed to each family every two months. The rubbery omelettes and puddings that it produced were ironically compared to linoleum tiles.

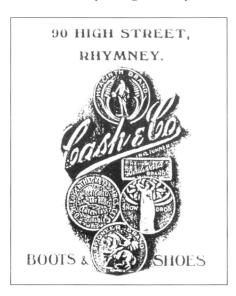

71. Glencross and Sons, situated on the High Street at the Royal Square, provided a veritable cornucopia of ironmongery and general goods. Seen here during the war years, with a road in front, yet to receive a Tarmac surface, it was to continue its business activities under the family name until the 1980s.

43

CHAPTER 3
Religion and Choirs

72. St David's Parish Church was built of local stone in the Doric style in 1842 with a chancel, nave and bell-tower containing one bell. Five further bells were installed, in 1875 in memory of Andrew Buchan, cast by John Warner & Sons of London. These were the 'sad bells of Rhymney' forever immortalised by poet Idris Davies and recognised world-wide through Pete Seager's composition which was sung by Bob Dylan. The Church's ecclesiastical parish was originally formed from the civil parish of Bedwellty, in the hundred (subdivision of a county having its own court) of Wentloog and County Court District of Tredegar. It came within the Blaenau Gwent division of the Abergavenny rural deanery, the Monmouth archdeaconry and the Llandaff diocese. The magnificent altar window of Our Lord's Ascension was presented to the Church by Andrew Buchan in 1856 in memory of his wife Sibella. Its organ was built by J W Walker of London and was installed in 1860 and the fine brass eagle lectern was presented in 1898 as a memorial to William Pritchard, the respected manager of the Company Shop. An altar desk stand and books were presented by Rees King in memory of his son Albert, a ministerial student who fell in the 1914-1918 war. The Church's register dates from 1843 which was when Alderman Copeland M.P., presented the church with its silver chalices. During this year was also built its associated vicarage at Nantllesg with an annual tithe charge of £200 but to be provided free as a gift to the vicar by the Rhymney Iron Company.

73. This was the St Matthews's Church Choir in about 1983, the young ladies sporting their Royal School of Church Music pendants. From top left, with vicar Brynmor Jones, are Choirmaster Tom Evans, Jonathan Morrissey, Gary Jones, lay-readers Terry Coleman and Mike Dunn and official lay-reader Norman Gilbert. In the second row, with Vicar's Warden Moelwyn Evans are to be seen Kim Prosser, Sara Gilbert, Gillian - , Catherine Jenkins, Peta Jones, Kathryn Jones and People's Warden Russell Jones. The third row consists of Gaynor Morgan, Diane Frowen, Michelle Chapman, Vicky James, Melanie Evans, Amanda Hook and in front, seated, are to be seen Nicola Evans, Sarah Dunn, Alison Jones, Kirsty Thomas, Katherine Hier and Nicola Rees.

74. The deacons of Penuel Chapel in the late 1960s were, from left to right standing, David Moseley, Aben Morris, Alcwyn Savage, Haydn Jones and Gareth Jones. Seated are John Jones, Tom Jenkins and Dai Savage.

75. Here we have the ladies choir of Penuel Chapel celebrating St. David's Day in the 1930s and suitably attired for the occasion. Deacons John Edwards and Iorwerth Edwards are to be seen on the left with conductor William John Jones on the right. Among the ladies have been identified Mary Jane Rees of Bryn Seion Street, Mrs Herriman of King Edward's Terrace, Madame Clement Jones of Queen's Crescent, Bessie Jones of Oakland Terrace and Mrs Savage of Gladstone Terrace.

45

76. This is the Sunday School class of Penuel Baptist Chapel that enjoyed a day's outing to Gilwern during the summer months of 1924. Sitting behind is Harry Beddoe and in the back row, from left to right, 'Shinken' Jenkins, Mary Jane Rees, Mary Ann Harris, Sarah 'Sal' Savage, Gladys Williams 'Pond Mawr', Nell Gunter (Bryn Seion), Mrs John, Mattie Jones and Willy Walters. In the front row are Mary Ann Savage, Greta Matthews, Mrs Richards (Alexandra), Ben Richards, Mrs George Young who emigrated to America and Rachel Williams.

77. Members of Jerusalem Chapel enjoy a reunion dinner in the 1960s. Among them are to be seen, with the Reverend and Mrs Beynon, Daniel James, Thomas 'Bacws', T J Williams, Owen Beddoe, W T Davies, Naomi Williams, Rebecca Williams, M A Young, Mrs A Lloyd, Mrs M Vaughan, Mrs Corns, Mrs A Lloyd, W Price, Owen, John Owen, W R Williams, J E Davies, Idris Owen, Vernita Owen, Mrs Narbed, Phyllis Davies, Mrs Jones, Mrs Phillips, Mrs Frances Price and Mrs B Griffiths.

78. The original Ebenezer Chapel was constructed in 1807 through the efforts of William Jones who induced ironmaster Benjamin Hall to grant a piece of land for this purpose. Jones was a tailor from Carmarthenshire who settled in Twyn Carno with his wife Esther Elias, both of whom were devoted Calvinistic Methodists. Through hard work his tailoring business soon grew large enough for him to employ nine assistants. Ebenezer Chapel was thereupon built at Twyn Carno and consisted of a hall measuring 30 feet by 20 feet with a pulpit, a small number of pews and a small burial ground attached. One of its first ministers was John Bevan (1770 - 1855) who became pastor of Ebenezer in 1811. So powerful was his hell-fire preaching throughout Gwent and Glamorgan that he was known to drive emotional and imaginative members of his congregation into a frenzy. The effect was to bring about a forceful revival in Calvinistic Methodism, a revival which carried his name as DIWYGIAD SHON BOWEN RHYMNI. Also a man of Carmarthenshire he was born and brought up on Maesgwastad Farm in the parish of Llanddeusant, the son of a chapel deacon where he, and his father, became greatly influenced by Williams Pantycelyn, 'The Sweet Singer of Wales'. The above photograph of a drawing by Rhymney artist Olwen Poole Hughes shows the original Ebenezer Chapel which was converted into a Welsh school and living accommodation following construction of the new chapel.

79. The growing Methodist congregation soon became too large for their small chapel and, in 1849, was built nearby the new Ebenezer Chapel shown aside. Its fabric was of local stone which was dug and brought by hand from the bed of the Rhymney River by devoted members of the congregation. Among those who toiled in this way for their faith were Samuel and Enoch Jones, the grandfather and uncle of the eminent Dr. Tom Jones, CH., who once lived at 100, High Street.
He was the father of Lady Irene White.

47

80.   The early non-conformist groups each had their own doctrine and standards of behaviour and the Calvinistic Methodists were known to be austere and conservative and laid great emphasis on teaching. Their ministers were said to be the best educated in Wales. Ebenezer Chapel in Twyn Carno maintained this doctrine by opening the first Welsh School in the town with its chapel elders acting as the School Board and participating in lessons. Above is shown the members of the Board in 1908 who were, from left to right in the back row, D Morgan, D Davies, Owen E Evans and D Jones the School Clerk. Seated are D Watkins, Thomas E Jones and Chairman D W Davies.

81.   A great servant of Calvinistic Methodism in Rhymney was David Jones, chief organist, conductor and deacon of Ebenezer for many years. By day he worked as a coal weigher in his office near the Eisteddfod Field where he decided when workmen's homes should receive their privilege loads of Company coal. Out of work he became Dewi Carno, essayist, musician, story-writer and raconteur. Dewi Carno (Davy Jones), 1869 - 1938, lived first at 1, Cambrian Street and then at Islwyn Terrace at the bottom of Price Street and was to develop into one of the most prolific writers that Rhymney has known. His eisteddfod successes were numerous and his twelve published essays ranged through such subjects as 'Education and Character in Wales' (1921), 'Devotion in Welsh Singing' (1924), 'Music and Morals' (1921), 'Sacred Music in Wales' (1925) and Music and Musicians of South Wales 1700 to 1928 (1928). He played as piano accompanist in dozens of concerts, composed anthems for children and for a time was the accompanist to two of the great choirs of Rhymney, John Price's United Choir and Daniel Owen's Male Voice Choir.

82. Early Methodist preaching in Rhymney and Pontlottyn, through the establishment of Ebenezer Chapel in 1807, was conducted strictly in Welsh and was further protective of the Welsh language through the later formation of its Welsh School. Many of the population of the area, however, were non-Welsh speaking and this in some respects provided a dilemma to those who wished to pursue the Calvinistic Methodist faith. Their answer came in 1894 when they established their own centre of prayer with the construction of the Victoria Calvinistic Methodist Church, shown above, on land bought from the Rhymney Iron and Coal Company. Here they conducted prayers until 1942 after which they united with the congregation of Brynhyfryd Calvinistic Chapel on Mount Pleasant. Their chapel building was then used by the Rhymney Town Band for practice sessions after which it was bought and became the venue of the Alcama Players, a local dramatic society which exhibited its talents with enthusiasm and charitably donated its proceeds to local needy organisations. "Alcama" means "tin" and it was at this time that the building adopted its nickname the "Tin Chapel" which it retained for many years. In 1961, almost twenty years after the Chapel had last rang to the sound of Calvinist teachings, a group of a dozen Christians, through the driving force of pastor David John Williams and his supportive wife Rosalie, covenanted together to re-establish the Church within the town. After four years they had purchased the now badly neglected building and its surrounding land and set about completely renovating it and restoring it to its original state. They named their new centre of prayer Calvary Chapel and here they revived the Calvinistic Methodist confession of faith from when the original church was established in 1894.

83. Here we see some of the congregation of the Calvary Chapel in about 1990 with, from the back, Mrs K Wilkins, Joan Heath, Janet Walters, Paula Jayne Gardner, Ann Gardner, Yvonne Heath, Hannah Lewis, Rosalie Williams with husband pastor David John Williams, Olwen Cunningham, Marj. Williams, Ethel Williams, Trevor Williams, Enid Hiscox, Eddie Hiscox and Meyrick Crandon.

84. The smiles on the faces of the officers of Jerusalem Chapel in 1985 also epitomize the relief that they feel on the successful opening of their new place of worship. One year earlier their chapel was found to be structurally unsafe and they were faced with a bill of £50,000 to put it right, a sum unfortunately well beyond the reach of the ageing congregation. Members were determined, however, that their church should continue to function for future generations and they decided that the vestry should be converted into a new chapel. The original chapel had stood for 144 years and was built in 1841 by members of the Zoar Chapel of Pontlottyn and there was great sadness at its dismantling. The new chapel was duly dedicated to a packed congregation and services, much to the joy of members, continue on the site. Pictured outside the new Jerusalem Chapel are, from left to right, deacon Ronald Jones, senior deacon John Evan Jones, secretary Morfydd Prytherch, minister Hadyn Jones, deacon Margaret Monk and treasurer Richard Blayney. Mr Jones holds a collecting plate that was carved from one of the pillars of the old pulpit.

85. Here we have the deacons of Jerusalem Chapel in 1957. In the back row, from left to right, are John Evan Jones, John Monk, Islwyn Owen, Mervyn Narbed and Idris Owen. Seated are Daniel James, Thomas John Williams, Reverend Glyndwr Richards, Owen Beddoe and William Thomas Davies.

86. The successful Rhymney Silurian Singers in the Angel Hotel, Abergavenny, happily display their trophy after winning the second male voice choir competition at the National Eisteddfod in 1958. The choir consisted of, from left to right in the back row, Thomas H Davies, Harry Breen, Terry Coleman, Ken Birch, Ray Morgan, Ray Williams, George Rees, Alun Moseley, Idris Davies, Dewi Morgan, George Googe, Bill Gurney, Fred Jones and Idris Jones. In the third row are Berwyn Moseley, Thomas Jones, John Emlyn Moseley, Emrys Prytherch, Bert Cumpstone, Trevor Jenkins, Trevor Harris, Griff Jones and Emrys Lloyd. In the second are to be seen Jack Rist, David Morgan, Gareth Jones, Bill Davies, Bill Pulman, Aeron John, Bob Jones, Thomas Martin Jones, Evan Hopkins, Robert Jones, John Davies and Edmund Williams. Seated in front are Idwal Jones, Thomas Williams, Phil Griffiths, Secretary Gwyn Jones, Musical Director Glynne Jones, Accompanist Myfanwy Jones, Bob Wilson, Reg Davies and Bill Worthington.

87. This is the Junior School Choir of Rhymney Grammar School that competed in the 3rd Urdd Eisteddfod in 1946 at Treorchy Junior School. It was the under 15 competition entitled 'Nant y Mynydd' and conducting the choir was music master Ken Richards accompanied by Margaret Lewis. Among the front row can be seen Myfanwy Herriman, Bronwen Jones, Gill Evans, Elizabeth Matthews, Valerie Thomas, Mary Jones, Jean Jones, Eira Morgan and Thelma Barnard. Among those behind are seen Sheila Jones, Barbara Theophilus, Mary Moseley, Beris Jones, Norma Gower, Mary Jones, Mary Davies, Sally Coonick, Eirwen Williams, Cynthia Jones, Jean Woods, Barbara Trump, Fay Burridge, Brenda Middleton, Eileen Fishlock, Sheila Lloyd and Sarah Anne Jones.

88. Rhymney Ladies Choir was formed in November 1950 and held its first practice in Twyn Carno Chapel with Tom Emlyn Owen as its conductor. Its first major success came in August 1956 when it gained first place in the National Eisteddfod at Aberdare. This led to a broadcast at St David's Hall and many concerts, including one at the Victoria Hall where one of the soloists happened to be a young tenor called Stuart Burrows. The second high in the choir's history was yet another first prize at the National Eisteddfod, this time in August 1960 at Cardiff under the leadership of T J Harris, to be followed the next day by a television appearance. On the retirement of T J Harris, Ralph Williams conducted the choir for ten years accompanied by Arthur Eynon and successes at eisteddfodau continued with wins at Cwmbran, Kington and Porthcawl but the hat-trick of Nationals continued to elude them. The National winners at Aberdare in 1956 are shown above with conductor Tom Emlyn Owen and accompanist Miss B M Davies. Among the smiling faces can be seen, behind, Mair Gurney, Nancy Worthington, Doris Short, Annie Williams, Ceinwen Williams, Mrs Poleman, Nancy Jones, Gwen Harris, Novella Benjamin, Katie Rich, Bessie 'The Ras' Williams, Miss Rees, Kitty Davies, Beatrice May Davies and Margaret Jones. Among the front row can be seen Lena Davies, Arianwen Williams, Mrs Harris, Margaret (Llangerrig), Blodwen Morris, Hattie Williams, Mrs Davies, Pauline Isaac and Anne Jane Brown.

89. Here we have a Joint Churches production of an operetta which was held in the Parish Hall, High Street in the late 1940s. Distinctively assembled in the back row can be seen John Hughes, Dai Lewis and George Evans. Among the middle row are Cyril Williams, Meidwen Parry, Betty Morgan, Daniel Ferguson, Iris Lewis, John Protheroe, Rees Parry, Edward Williams and seated in front can be seen Mair Parry.

CHAPTER 4

Education and Sport

The only purpose-built school that still remains in Rhymney today as a relic of the 'Old Rhymney' is the Upper Rhymney Infants School which was constructed following the 1870 Education Act near Penuel Chapel. School life a century or more ago would be unrecognisable today with the computer having replaced the bead-frame and with finger-touch central heating instead of the open-hearth coal fire or the cast iron stove. Children then wore clogs or heavy leather boots, hob-nailed with studs and metal plates hammered in on the familiar hobbing iron, repairs often being undertaken by parents. Girls wore thick black stockings, laced up boots and starched pinafores and boys knickerbocker suits with stiff white collars. Reading, writing and arithmetic were the basic subjects taught with some history and geography, but Welsh was strictly forbidden, neither taught nor spoken, and was seen as a hindrance to the child's progress in the English language. Children were virtually brainwashed at school, and often at home, into believing that no progress was possible in life unless English was taken as their first language and this philosophy persisted for many years. Those who spoke Welsh in the classroom were shamed by being made to wear the 'Welsh Note', a knotted rope around their neck to which was tied a piece of wood. A token of disgrace the 'Note', (often pronounced 'Not') was worn until another child slipped up and transgressed by uttering a word of Welsh in which case the rope and wood was transferred to his neck. The Welsh language was therefore necessarily sustained through religious institutions, bible-readings, chapel schools, festivals, drama groups and societies.

Earlier schools before the Education Act of 1870 were set up by voluntary societies. The National School Society, supported by the Rhymney Ironworks, built such schools as the Office School near to what is now the railway station, and the Middle Rhymney School which were run mainly on the religious principles of the Church of England and where, strictly, Welsh was not spoken. The British School Society, on the other hand, was mainly the domain of the Non-Conformists and their schools, such as the Upper Rhymney Primary in Cambrian Street and the Wellington School, were a progression from tuition in private dwellings and chapel vestries. Children attending these voluntary schools paid a weekly fee of 2d (1p) or 3d (1½p) according to their age and additional funding was earned by the ministers who managed the schools through lectures, evenings of entertainment and through government grants. The 1870 Education Act took responsibility for running the schools away from local ministers, much to their relief, and placed it in the hands of the Bedwellty Board. School fees were abolished and all children were then required to be given an elementary education and to attend school until they were thirteen years of age.

90. Physics-class students of Rhymney Grammar School enjoy a moment's respite on the playing field between lessons in 1955 with their physics master Norman Gilbert. From top left are to be seen Roy Evans, Glyndwr Jones, Lionel Symmonds, Brian Jones, In the middle row are James Oliver, Gwilym Richards, Dennis Perrott, Gareth Taylor and in front John Davies, Ann Jones and Anita Jones.

91. The children of Upper Rhymney Primary School, in around 1896, are immaculately attired in their starched pinafores, lace collars, black dresses and, of course, their hob-nailed boots. The school was, by then, run by the Bedwellty Board and among its staff were Jim 'Pompey' Shields, R S Morgan, J O Ingram, C G Thomas and W S Jenkins who created a major staffing problem when they were all conscripted for service in the Great War from 1914 to 1918, one never to return. Lady teachers at the time included Kate Olive Thomas, Katie (Jones) Morgan and M A Thomas, two of whom are to be seen in the photograph.

92. The young ladies of the Middle Rhymney Mixed School in the early 1900s pose in their Sunday best for their school photograph. Their school was built at the bottom of Manest Street in 1858 at a cost of £3000 by the Rhymney Iron Company and replaced an earlier one that had been destroyed by fire soon after its construction. This was the time of slates and chalk, before the ink-well but after the sand-tray when a shallow tray of sand was used for writing on using a sharpened piece of wood.

93. Rhymney Lower Infants School wedged between Plantation Street and Jerusalem Street (originally known as Dockers Terrace), was opened in 1882, and cost the princely sum of £500 to build. School dinners were then unheard of and children took their own lunches to eat, the poorer ones often having to make do with a chunk of bread, a lump of cheese and a flask of cold tea. From the earlier times of voluntary schooling children were for months on end not permitted to attend school by their parents because they were able, at a very early age, to work in iron and coal mines and augment the family income. If there was a strike the classrooms were known to suddenly fill with an influx of such children who only stayed as long as the strike lasted or until their parents found them other work to do. This was much to the chagrin of the teaching staff who were faced with the chaos and disruption that was brought to their classrooms. George Berry Kovachich at the Upper Rhymney School brought it home with his log entry in January 1873 which read 'Most of them are as wild as the "untaught Indian's brood", and, 'School noisy. The uncouth savages from the mines do not appear to know the simplest form of decency'

94. An inside classroom of the Lower Rhymney Infants School showing the firm discipline that was imposed on the young pupils who were required to sit erect with arms behind their backs. Children sat at wooden desks which had a shelf underneath, the seats fixed to the desk with cast iron bars. All teachers had canes which, in many cases, were liberally used to teach in an atmosphere of fear and lessons were learnt by chanting tables, poetry and other subjects over and over again. Most names for the above 1926 photograph of children of the Lower Rhymney Infants School have been kindly provided by David John Williams. Among those in the front row, from left to right, are to be seen Tony Bisi, Nora Hill, Moira Jones, Gwyneth Williams, Betty Moseley and Ralph Jones. In the second row up are David Evans, Tom Sims, Marie McCarthy, Olga Salmon, Rosie Watkins, Mildred Griffiths and David John Williams. Third row up can be seen David Smout, Doreen Williams, Alice Price, Eve Clark, Gweneth Williams and Jackie Williams. Among the back group are to be seen Gilbert John, Emrys Jenkins, John Alfred Thomas, Doris Robins and Haydn Gwilym.

95. In a more enlightened age the nine-year-olds of Upper Rhymney Junior School in 1973 seem positively radiant. With schoolmistress Margaret Phillips and Headmaster Emrys Howells are to be seen, from top left in the back row, Jeffrey Norris, Gary Worgan, Ian Weaver, Richard Davies, Anthony Evans, Carl Pearce, Ian Morgan, In the middle row are Tracey Williams, Julie Morgan, Vicky Hardacre, Sharon Edwards, Joy Yandle, Beverly Davies, Glynda Prosser and Lesley Powell and, in front, Carol Matthews, Debbie Morris, Joanne Walters, Maria Watts, Helen Moseley, Alison Davies and Ann Hughes. The two lads in front are Huw Thomas and Christopher Price.

96. Enjoying a Nativity presentation at Christmas in 1984 are children of the Upper Rhymney Infants School. The 'conifers' in the back row, from the left, are Kelly Griffiths, Lisa Matthews, Leanne Price, Stephanie McMahon, Donna Evans, Tracey Jones, Rebecca Eynon, Emma Williams and Claire Richards. In the middle row are Sharon James, Zoe Williams, Matthew Burr, Catherine Owen, Sarah Vest, Rhian Morgan, Huw Davies, Simon Lewis and Matthew Rowlands. In front are Andrew Rowlands, Jason Davies, Jamie Boudana, Jamie Butler, Gavin Evans, Lee Davis and Paul Edwards.

97. The Lower Sixth of Rhymney Grammar School in 1951 where we see, in the back row, Granville Marshall, Howard Price, Raymond Jones, Kay Tolfree, Norman Ogbourne, John Berry Jones and John Harrison. Seated, from left to right, are Gill Evans, Christine Hiscox, Valerie Thomas, Welsh mistress Doris Short, Merle Thomas, Alma Lloyd and Fay Burridge.

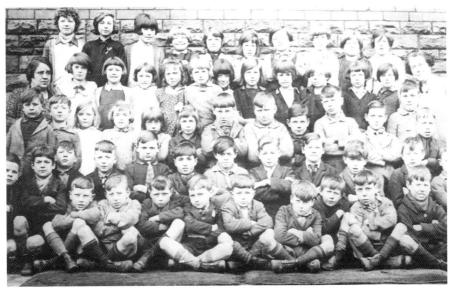

98. This 1928 photograph of children of the Lower Rhymney Junior School must surely contain many grandparents of people still living in the town. Through the remarkable memory of Rosalie Williams we are able to give many of the children's names in the hope that readers may be able to make identifications. In the back row, from left to right we have Betty Jones, Miss Samuel, Ivy Edwards, Irene Purcell, Master Martin, unknown, Miss May, Joan Baker, May Keefe and Rosie Faulkner. Second row down, with teachers Miss Jones and Miss Perkins, can be seen Jenny Jones, Nancy Hughes, Iris Lodwick, Miss Bayliss, Beryl Mail, Ira Griffiths, Envis Davies, Phyllis Pritchard, Doris Spriggs, Nancy Williams and Betty Davies. In the third row from the top are Jacky Jones, Terry Hawkins, Mary Middleton, Rosalie Lewis, Maureen Boucher, Doreen Llewellyn, unknown, Billy Jones, Bill Price, unknown, Master Evans, Billy Hewlett and Master Burston. Below are then seen Billy Acreman, Andrew Davage, Master Evans, John Evans, Master Jones, Billy Fradd, Ivor (Boy) Jenkins and Tommy Roberts.

99. When the Rhymney Grammar School, The Lawn, opened its doors in 1924 the sum total of its teaching staff was four, under headmaster Thomas Price. Above, in 1963, we see headmaster Stan Lloyd with his team of teachers who are, from left to right balanced precariously in the back row, David Llewellyn, Les Aubrey, Ron James, John Williams, John Smith, Wilfred Williams, Brian Watkins and Neville Browning. Islwyn Atkinson, Gwyn Davies, Havis Wood, Norman Gilbert, Ralph Williams, author Marion Evans, Marion Holder and Heulwyn Eynon are in the next row down. In the second row from the front are Jim Brewer, Mrs D T Williams, Dilys Price, Mrs Atkinson, Angela Savage, Miss Jones, Margaret Vines, Monica Davies and Meidwen (Parry) Davies. Seated are to be seen Nesta Bell-Richards, Doris Short, Evan Hopkins, Stan Lloyd, Marjorie Sutton, Mary Evans and Anita Gardner Jones.

100. The staff of the Upper Rhymney Junior School in the 1930s at a time when women, akin with many other occupations from the year 1909, were not allowed to be in the teaching profession if married. In the back row are Bessie Jones of Oakland Terrace, Isaac (Ike) Herriman of King Edward's Terrace, Tommy James, Morgan Gronow, and Elizabeth 'Bacus' Davies. Among the front row seated alongside headmaster D G Lloyd are to be seen Susie Jones of Colenso Terrace, Phillis Owen Jones and James E Williams of Alexandra Place. Also seen is Jenny Cuthbert Evans who died this year aged 104.

101. A 1950 class of the Lower Rhymney Junior School, The Wellington, with teachers Tegwyn Jones and Jack Richards. Some pupils to be seen are, in the top row, Alan Pugh, John Evans, Alun Davies and David Welsh; in the second row Brenda Chapell, Brenda Walters, Jean Barry, Janice Williams, Joan Baker, Geraldine Coughlin and Marilyn Walters. In front, seated, can be seen Albert Lester, Keith Bromage, Eifion Owen, Rosemary Parry, Carol Morris, Jean Perry, Brian Roberts, Norman Moseley and Clive Jones.

102. Here we have the mixed school choir of the 5th and 6th forms of Rhymney Grammar School in 1960. In the back row are, from left to right, Gerald Williams, Jeffrey Morgan, Terry Baker, Tom Purnell, Colin Jones, Emlyn Jones, John Ison and John Grey. Below are to be seen Neville Jones, Gloria Davis, Marion Philpott, Eileen Harrington, Avril Moseley, Gillian Harris, Geraint Jones, Pat Jones, Rosalind Watkins, Hetty Taylor, Valmai Llewellyn, Ursula Stockman and Maxim Morgan. Next row down are Clive Jones, Peter Jones, Margaret Eynon, Mary Beatrice Jones, Kay Evans, Pat Breen, Margaret Powell, Avril Roberts, Pam Middleton, Janis Benjamin, Roberts Griffiths and music teacher Ken Richards. Among the front row are Linda Cox, Glayne Howells, Sheila Eynon and Heulwyn Moseley.

103. Here we have Maynard Vaile's class of the Upper Rhymney Junior School in 1973, seen with headmaster Emrys Howells. In the top row, from left to right, are Glenda Prosser, Barry Davies, Richard Davies, Carl Pearce, Anthony Evans, Ian Weaver and Joanne Walters. Next row down are Julie Morgan, Sharon Edwards, Vicky Hardacre, Joy Yandle, Tracey Barnard, Beverley Davies and Ann Hughes. Seated are Helen Moseley, Maria Watts, Jackie Theophilus, Carol Matthews, Jill Lewis, Alison Davies and Lesley Power. In front, cross-legged, are Jeffrey Norris, Gary Worgan, Chris Price, Ian Morgan and Robert Davies.

104. This is the Wellington School Recorder Group in 1950 that proudly entertained the public in the James Smith Hall at a Festival of Britain celebration evening. From left to right, standing, are Avril Mumford, Melba Harris, Kay Bromage, Ann Mudway, Jennifer Davies, Jennifer Howells, Diane Wilding, Janet Perry and Betty Howes. Seated are Godfrey Davies, Dilwyn Moseley, Jeanette Fear, Ralph Williams, Maureen Watkins, Anne Jones and Adrian Edwards.

105. The Rhymney Grammar School choir in 1951 pose outside the gymnasium with music teacher Ken Richards. Most names have been found so please excuse any omissions. The back row, from left to right, consists of Marina Dallenegra, - , Jean Watkins, Marina Davies, Betty Wilding, Betty Davies, Morfydd Davies, Barbara Cleaves, Gwyneth Williams, Pamela Jones, Margaret Evans, - , Marion Davies, Sylvia Weaver, Irene Jones, Wendy Small, Marion Jones, Joan Mudway, Myfanwy Herriman, In the middle row are Merle Thomas, Eleanor Bebb, Kay Tolfree, Eirwen Williams, - , Bronwen Jones, Hilary Ogborne, Shirley Gray, Desdemona Barnard, Ann Hill, Cynthia Jones, Catherine Roach, Sarah Jones, Norma Gower, Freda Neagle, Alma Lloyd, Sheila Lloyd and Fay Burridge. In the front row are to be seen Maureen Morris, - , Shirley Palmer, - , Gladys Cleaves, Janet Lodwick, Connie Viney, Sylvia Newell, Ken Richards, Sonia Weeks, Thelma Barnard, Ray Jones, Jean Davies, - , - , Maureen McMahon and Valerie Thomas.

106. Students' prize-giving day for Rhymney Grammar School in 1956 was held in the Parish Hall, High Street. Working from the front row backwards are to be seen Judy Small, Kay Evans, Eileen Harrington, Jean Davies. In the second row are Beth Harris, Myfanwy Williams, Janette Rogers, Lynette Thomas and Mair Joseph. Further behind are Janet Price, Lindy Small, Sheila Eynon, Jillian Harris, Catherine Rees, Janet Jones, Angela Davies, Ursula Stockman, Mary Moseley, Heulwen Moseley, Morfydd Jones, Nesta Bell Richards, Meidwen Parry, Nita Gardner Jones, Gwyneth Wathan, Margaret Prytherch, Marjorie Sutton, Idris Jones, Carl Barnard, Norman Moseley, John Howes, Roger Phillips, Danny Hale, Philip Rees, Ralph Williams and Robert Woods.

107. Another prize-giving session, on this occasion the boys' section in 1952 in Twyn Carno Chapel. Among the group, are to be seen Billy Davies, Keith Dunhill, John Evans, Alun Williams, James 'Amos' Davies, Ian Barnard, Clive Jones, Charlie Baker, Alan Pugh, John Carberry, Byron Thomas, Gary Weaver, Ernie Weaver, Mervyn James, Godfrey Davies, Philip Rees, Ralph Williams, Derek Hoare, John Baker, Harvard Evans, Royden Powell, Glyn Meredith, Baynham Morgan, Craig Brewer, Cyril Weaver, Robert Jones, Eddie Thomas, Gareth Owen, Malcolm Jones and schoolmistress Morfydd Jones.

108. Class 3 of Upper Rhymney Junior School in the year 1970, with schoolmaster Tom Williams and headmaster Dai Hughes, consisted of, in the back row from left to right, Shaun Jones, Nigel Welsh, Lesley Hogan, Brenda Theophilus, Carol Williams, Susan Warley, Christine Davies, Stephen Lloyd and Linda Williams. Next row down are Byron Davies, Thomas Baker, Susan Evans, Gillian Brown, Pat Faulkner, Sandra Moon, Carl Harris, Dianne Evans and Paul Morgan. Among the second row, seated, are Kim Williams, Susan Carter, Wendy Richards, Rhian Walters, Christine Ball and Vivienne Williams. In the front row can be seen Malcolm Richards, Nigel Collier, John Moon and Christopher Llewellyn.

109. With Mathematics teacher Stan Lloyd, Headmaster J D C Anthony and English teacher Marjorie Sutton are the Rhymney Grammar School prefects for the year 1960 - 1961. In the back row, from left to right, we have Geraint Williams, Norman Moseley, Peter Jones, Emlyn Williams, Neville Jones, John Ison, John Gray, Tom Purnell, Clive Jones, Jeffrey Harrington. In the middle row are Hettie Taylor, Rosalind Watkins, Eileen Harrington, Pat Jones, Margaret Eynon and Pat Breen. In front Kay Evans, Linda Cox, Glayne Howells, Astra Lewis, Maxim Morgan, Valmai Llewellyn, Olwen Edwards and Ursula Stockman.

110. A class of the Lower Rhymney Junior School in around 1949. In the back row with school secretary Josie Cusack can be seen Anita Withers, Melba Harris, Louvaine Rowlands, Ann Williams, Ann Mudway, Janet Parry, Jean Matthews, Elizabeth Lewis and Diane Wilding, followed by schoolmistress Muriel Henry. Among the second row can be seen Pat Morris, Kay Bromage, Betty Howes and Ann Beddoe. In front can be seen Dorian Williams, David Price, Derek Pugh, John Price, Alan Morgan, Maxim Morgan and Alan Cunningham.

111. The Upper 6th Form of Rhymney Grammar School pose outside the gymnasium with English teacher Marjorie Sutton in the summer of 1951. Standing, from left to right, are Illtyd Clement Thomas, Henry Matthews, Tudor Wyndham Roberts, Cynthia Elizabeth Jones, Kathleen Elizabeth Roche, Sheila Lloyd, John Keith Bassett, Gerald Downey and Richard John Maunder. Seated are Mary Moseley, Bronwen Jones, Jean Jones, Miss M Sutton, Thelma Barnard, Norma Gower and Sarah Anne Jones.

112. Children of Ysgol Cymraeg Rhymni in 1976 when the school was situated at the bottom of Goshen Street. Among those in the back row are to be seen Helen Morris, Cathryn Evans, Nicola Colbeck, Remo John, Melanie Colbeck. In the middle row with schoolmistress Heulwen Williams can be seen Gerwyn Parfitt, Jonathan Jones, Helen Moseley, Ian John, David Samuels, Eryl John, Ruth Moseley, Nicola Evans and Moira Davies with teachers June Yates and Dilys Young on the end. Among the front row are Wyn Evans, Huw Davis, Alcwyn Savage, two young Sibley brothers, Helen Rogers, Paula Gardner, Rhian Moseley, Julie Williams and Rhian Davies.

113. At an earlier date, in around the early 1950s, we show a nursery class of the Welsh School, with staff, that was run on a Saturday morning basis. In the back row are to be seen Welsh teachers Rita Owen and Heulwen Williams, parents Rhiannon Williams and Onwy Beynon, School Secretary Bob Roberts, Morwena Evans, Beatrice May Davies and Tess Francis. Children, from left to right in the back row, are Brian James, Malcolm Jones, Myra Evans, Anwen Morgan, Ann Williams, Margaret Rist, Margaret Prytherch, Glayne Howells, Vivienne Francis, Elizabeth Williams, Linda Evans, Robert Howells and Lyn Owen. Next row down are Edward Rist, Alan Wharton, Judith Davies, Gail Davies, Mary Rees, Rhian Jones, Eurona Griffiths, Buddug and Naomi Williams. In front can be seen Iwan Lloyd, David Rees, Hefin Jones, Huwan Williams and, behind and in front of this row, Sheila Williams, Eluned Prytherch, Avril Roberts, Huw Beynon, Ann Evans, Ruth Francis, Rhoda Williams, Janet Price, Macgwen Davies, Nesta Howells, Meryl Thomas, Gwyn Howells, Nesta Young, Dennis Humphries and Barry Hughson.

114. Above and below we have two classes of Upper Rhymney Junior School involved in celebrations for the Queen's Jubilee in 1977. Above is Class 3a with teacher Dewi Williams and headmaster Phil Griffiths and in the back row can be seen Mark Lloyd Williams, Paul Beddoe Jones, Paul Baxter, Jonathan Evans, Julian Jones, Andrew Lewis and Tristan Thomas. In the second row down are to be seen Ian Shepherd, Mark Williams, Jane Challenger, Angela Morgan, Tracey Kearn, Martyn Prosser and Paul Davies. Seated front can be seen Rhian James, Helen Edwards, Bethan Phillips, Selina Davies, Lyn George, Jayne Mobberly and Catherine Clark and in front, cross-legged are Gary Perrin, Timothy Jones, Paul Cuss, David Thomas and Gerald Hollis.

115. This is Class 3 with teacher Graham Evans and again head Phil Griffiths. In the back row are Stephen Jones, David Edwards, Steven Parry, Simon Jones, David Lester, Carl Thomas and Colin Rudd. The middle row includes Rebecca Davies, Jacqueline Lawrence, Kathryn Jones, Cerys Ward, Michael Moon and Christopher Sullivan. Seated front are to be seen Beverley Wooley, Gillian Watkins, Mandy Lawrence, Mandy Jones, Sharon Moss, Suzanne Pearce, Gail Worgan and Leanne Thomas and on the floor are Anthony Paul Jones, Darren Mutton, Mark Watts, Michael Evans and Wayne Simms.

116. Rhymney Comprehensive School pupils with form master Ralph Williams, pose in 1962 for their annual photograph in the gymnasium. From top left are to be seen Susan Greeves, Gaynor Richards, Keith Parry, Janet Powell, John Roberts, David Prosser, Adrian Jackson, unsure, and Jayne Sheen. In the middle row are Michael Jones, Carol Austin, Linda Evans, Pamela Bushell, Rosemarie Flannagan, Geraint Gallop, Keith Jarman and Jeanette Price. Seated, front, can be seen Martin Powell, Gwilym Roberts, Ann Morris, Cheryl Powell, Michael Williams, Billy Llewellyn, Malcolm Aeron, Lynne Theophilus and Phillip Williams. Cross-legged are Diane Thomas, Alun Austin and David Price.

117. Here we have the first and second year Form VI prefects of the Rhymney Grammar School in the year 1965/66. In the back row, from left to right, are Lynda Vaughan, Margaret Jones, Keith Davies, Neil Protheroe, Ieuan Moseley, Penny Edwards and Janice Collins. Seated are John Lambert, head boy Huw Davies, Marjorie Sutton, English teacher, Headmaster Stan Lloyd, Deputy Head Evan Hopkins, head girl Sylvia Williams and Pamela Wiltshire. In front are Ann Evans and Margaret Williams.

118. These are children of the Upper Rhymney Infants School in 1969. In the back row, from left to right with schoolmistress Marion Philpots, are Alan Jones, Huw Thomas, Keith Thomas, Billy Barnard, Martyn Bird, Dean Hancock, Carl Davies, Colin Williams, Brian Rees and David Morris. In the middle are Jill Jury, Kim Greaves, Jillian Thomas, Linda Elias, Anthony Evans, Mike Harris, Sharon Edwards, Sally Lane, Linda Knight with head teacher Mrs Williams. In front are Beverly Jones, Alison Davies, Maria Watts, Paula Penny, Angela Knight, Joanne Walters, Jill Thomas and Maria Stephens.

119. Middle Rhymney schoolchildren celebrate St David's Day in 1931 with a fine array of hats and shawls. Standing at the back are schoolmaster Eddie Jones and headmaster Jim 'Pompey' Shields. In the earlier days of the school, when parents paid fees for their children to attend, pupils were taught a wide range of domestic subjects and produced goods that were sold to help fund the running of the school. Sewing, needlework, broadside stitching, weaving and spinning, embroidery work, crocheting, pointwork and broderie anglais were taught to the girls and woodwork, shoe and clog-making and leatherwork taught to the boys. This was a widespread activity throughout schools of this standard some of which, such as the Upper Rhymney School, were supported by the Haberdashers Society. Most boys, on leaving school, went into the mines and the girls into domestic service.

120. The prefects of Rhymney Secondary Grammar School in 1962 are photographed outside the school gymnasium. From top left are Trevor Thompson, Bernard Morrissey, Colin Davies, Phillip James, Graham Williams, Gary Hulbert and John Neagle. Seated are Lorrainne Carey, Hazel Williams, Eira Richards, schoolmistress Morfydd Jones, headmaster Mr J D C Anthony, sportsmaster Havis Wood, Meryl Williams, Christine Phillips and Barbara Harris.

121. The Upper Rhymney Junior School football team in 1974 were, from top left, Robert Williams, Malcolm Turner, Darren Matthews, Anthony Evans, Steven Price, Graham Jones, Kevin Matthews and Malcolm Evans. Seated are Ian Weaver, Gareth Jones, Philip Evans, Carl Davies and Gary Worgan.

122. The children of Standard 3 of Lower Rhymney Council School pose outside their school in 1930 with their teachers Barbara Jones and Kitty Davies. The headmaster at the time was David Matthews and other staff Dai Hughes and Emrys Taylor of Carn y Tyla Terrace Abertysswg. Thanks to the excellent memory of Howard Evans, who then lived in Hill Street, most names are available. In the back row, from left to right, are Ralph Williams, Sam Lester, Howard Evans, David Evans, Berwen Thomas, Emlyn Powells, David Narbed, Tom George, David Smout, Harry Miller, Tony Bisi, Ronald Davies and Tom Johns. Some second row names are Annie Powell, - , Gladys Williams, Nora Clark, Miss Williams, Olga Salmon, Enid Williams, Miss Price, Doris Robins, - , - . In the next row down are Miss Williams, Miss Griffiths, Olwen Davies, - , Mary Hannah Thomas, Phyllis Jenkins, Florence Dunkerton, Annie Lloyd, - , Mary Morgan, - , Miss Morris, - , - and Miss Davies. Crosslegged on the yard floor are Russell Richards, Mervyn Powell, Master Otley, David Williams, Emrys Jenkins, Raymond Evans, Tom Walsh, Jack Llewellyn, John Alfred Thomas, Ronald Davies, Tom Bell Powell and Jakie Williams.

123. Here we have the Urdd Gobiath Cymru group of the Rhymney Secondary School in their 1933/34 year. Among them are to be seen Doris Mayle, Thelma Gardner, Iris Hill, Prudence Birmingham, Betty Wellings, John S Evans, Glyn Richards, William Morris and Doug Hughes together with schoolmistress Miss Muriel Henry.

124. The Rhymney Grammar School Cricket XI in 1960 consisted of, from top left, Jeffrey Morgan, Tom Purnell Geraint Jones, Jeffrey Harrington, Emlyn Davies, Robert Griffiths with schoolmaster Dai Llewellyn. Seated are Colin Jones, Terry Baker, Maxim Morgan, Clive Jones, Lyn Roberts, John Beddoe and Robert Woods.

125. The girls' netball team of the same year were Avril Roberts, Margaret Powell, Pam Williams, and Astra Lewis. In front, with sportsmistress Francis Jones, are **unknown**, Jean Loach, Valmai Llewellyn and Hetty Taylor.

126. The first mini-rugby team of the Upper Rhymney Junior School pose, ready for action, during their 1974-75 year. Among the back row can be seen Glyn Cummings, Julian Moseley, Mark Jones, Ian Pulsford and Mark Faulkner and, among the front, Steven Moseley, Gareth Jones, Anthony Evans and Gary Owen.

127. The aspiring netball team of the Upper Rhymney Junior School in 1977 consisted of, in the back row, Alison Davies, Angela Evans, Joy Yandle and Zoe Jones. Sitting are Mary Davies, Marina Thomas, Lesley Powell, Wendy Drury and Jill Lewis.

128. This is one that may trigger the memory of some of the older generation of Lower Rhymney. It is a young Emrys Taylor's class of the Lower Rhymney Primary School, then a Council School, in 1930. By courtesy of the magnificent memory of Hilda Davies most of the names have been made available. Among the top row, from left to right, are Harry Gittens, Tommy Morgan, Frankie Smith, Billy Roper, Gwilym Harding, Glyn Williams, Bobby Sims, Ryddyd Pugh, Cyril Perry and Billy Acreman. Next row down are to be seen Millie Pearce, Margaret Davies, Mary John, Mair Howells, Olive Jones (?), Marie Hughes, Iris Hill, Enid Hemmings, Doreen Williams, Lilly Moberley, Harriet Margaret Powell and Jenny Thomas. Third row down are Rene Davies, Betty Moseley, Margaret Greaney, Violet Bishop, Connie Tozer, Martha John, Nancy Hall, Eileen Buckley, Blod Davies, Muriel Davies, Dossie Yainton and Eileen Toomey and seated in front are Victor Jones, David Davies, Dewi Phillips, Wilfred Lambert, Ivy Kinsey, Hilda Davies, Sarah Spacey, Harold Potter, Hadyn Price, Gethin Thomas, Dai Bishop and Jenkin Moseley.

129. The Grammar School Cricket XI pose with sportsmaster Havis Woods before action in 1951. Standing are, from the left, Herbie Davies, Ron Magness, Brian Williams, Henry Matthews, Alun Cook, Richard Maunder and John Lloyd Williams. Seated are John D Jones, J W Evans, Roy Morgan, Tudor Roberts, Norman Ogbourne and Gerald Downey.

130. The 1957/58 school choir of Rhymney Grammar consisted of, with as many names as we could gather from top left, Beryl Wathan, Valerie Jones, Annette Crump, Kay Evans, Irona Isaacs, Janice Benjamin, Lynette Thomas, Olwen Jones, Ann Williams, Jean Davies, Pauline Jones, Sheila Smith, Judith Jenkins, Linda Cox, Myfanwy Williams, Melba Harris, Maureen Buckley, Nora Price, Vanda Small, Glayne Howells, Annwen Morgan, Heather Robins, Sonia Jones, Christina Barry, Rosemary Jones, Catherine Woods, Valerie Jenkins, Maureen Gallier, Maureen Watkins and Beth Harris. Music teacher Ken Richards is seen in the front row.

131. The girls' tennis team of the Grammar School in 1952 are shown here with Latin mistress Llewella Jones and Welsh mistress Doris Short. In the back row are Myfanwy Herriman, Sheila Lloyd, Kay Tolfree and Margaret Carey and seated Barbara Clease, Valerie Thomas and Helena Bebb.

74

132. In the early 1950s members of the Rhymney Boys' Club worked hard to put the finishing touches to their new clubhouse near Clarendon Row, the original Brewery Club. Taking a brief interlude for the cameraman are, from top left, David Williams, John Vaughan, Billy Davies, David Jones on the barrow and Havard Jones. Below are Billy Vaughan, Bernard Powell, Ray Vaughan and Ray Withers.

133. About the same time Penydre AFC continued a run of successful seasons with this 1955 team shown above. Three times Rhymney Valley League winners between 1955 and 1959 their headquarters was in the Castle Hotel where they washed in tin baths after each game. Their football pitch was at The Track at T'ai Level Lo. This particular team consisted of, from top left, Frank Harris, Ivor Price, Glan Evans, Billy Charles, Dick Price and 'Tot' Thomas. In front are Ron Price, Bryn Matthews, Ossie Cavender, Ken Gardner and Lyndon Goode.

134. A cheerful young lad of the town who was to excel in becoming one of Rhymney's sporting greats started his life as the son of a postmaster in Moriah Street in February 1940. A protégé of Rhymney Grammar School Berwyn Jones sprang on to the athletics scene when, as a schoolboy under the careful nurturing of sportsmaster David Llewellyn, he clocked ten seconds in the hundred yards and went on win the Monmouthshire Schoolboys senior 100 yards and 200 yards sprint events. His huge potential continued through college at Caerleon where, in 1959, he ran for Wales, setting long-standing records in the same events. A move from Caerleon to Loughborough College to take on additional qualifications in Physical Education saw Berwyn set up yet another record in the 100 yards of 9.7 seconds in 1961 and his selection for the University Athletics Union in the World Students Games in Sofia, Bulgaria, where he won the silver medal in the 100 metres event. In 1962 Berwyn left Loughborough to take a teaching post in Birmingham where his sporting career continued to move from strength to strength. He that year represented Wales in the Commonwealth Games in Perth, Australia and Great Britain in the European Championships at Belgrade. He became famous as a member of the Peter Radford and 'Three Joneses' relay team and he ran in athletics matches against the West Germans and Poles at the White City and the Norwegians in Bergen. The peak of Berwyn's athletics career, however, must be in 1963 when he set a new Welsh record of 9.5 seconds for the 100 yards to be followed by the A.A.A. title, the Cup for which he is seen holding above, so becoming the first Welshman in this century to have won this title. This was followed by a major success in August of that very eventful year when, as a member of the Great Britain Relay Team, he combined in beating the Americans at the White City in the 4 x 100 yards relay. Such a success had not been achieved for thirty years and, in doing so, the team, known internationally as 'The Flying Squad', set up a new British, European, Commonwealth and World record of 40 seconds. Tours of Russia and Hungary continued with the Great Britain team where further accolades were collected and with Berwyn taking new records in the 100 metres and relay events, ranking him number one in Europe and number three in the world over 100 metres. 1964 saw a huge turning point in the remarkable life of this Rhymney man who then made the decision to quit amateur athletics and to play rugby league as a professional with Wakefield Trinity. The gamble paid off and his sprinting and rugby union background, together with his immense competitiveness, stood him in good stead in a highly demanding and tough sport. So effective in fact was his impact that Berwyn, after only twenty five games with his new club, was chosen to play for the British Rugby League team against France. He was then selected in 1966 to tour Australia and New Zealand with the Great Britain Lions team where he ended up as top try-scorer with 27 tries in 15 games. He also played for Bradford Northern and finished his rugby league days with St Helens thereby concluding a sporting career that was both dazzling and inspiring. Berwyn then took a teaching post near the Welsh border at Ross-on-Wye where he now lives out his retirement with his wife Ann, no doubt sharing colourful memories of a highly charged career that must make him one of the greatest sportsmen that Rhymney has ever produced.

135. Away fixtures to West Wales and the West Country were always eagerly looked forward to for the enthusiastic and warm welcome that was given. This trip to Fishguard by the Rhymney Athletic rugby team was no exception. In the back row are to be seen Ted Thorpe, a 'loan' from the home team, Mike Dunn, Malcolm Rowlands, Cliff Cotterell, Gareth Davies, Bob Mutton, Des Colbeck, Howard Thomas, Huw Griffiths and bus-driver Malcolm Jones. In front, from left to right are Clayton Matthews (missing one shoe on return!), Philip Matthews, Captain Roy Evans, Norman Davies, Terry Baker and Geoff Brice who immortalized himself by, as full back, kicking a dropped goal from the halfway line.

136. The Rhymney Secondary Grammar School Junior XV in their 1955/56 season were, from the back row with sportsmaster Don Durham, Billy Davies, Billy Watkins, John 'Tosh', Maxim Morgan, Derek Hoare, John Baker, Ralph Williams, Charlie Baker and Carl Griffiths. In the second row are Mervyn James, Ian Barnard, Roy Oliver, Roger Phillips, Danny Hale, Ernie Weaver, Barry Shankland and Alan Williams, with, sitting in front, Norman Price and James Davies.

CHAPTER 5

People and Events

137. Described as 'a pillar of the Church and Welsh life in Rhymney', the Reverend Rhys Bowen was pastor of Moriah Welsh Congregational Church until his death in 1957 aged 58 years. Born in Brynamman in the Swansea Valley he began work in the mines but after matriculation became a student at University College, Cardiff, where he graduated with first-class honours in Welsh. He then went to the Memorial Theological College, Brecon, before becoming minister at Moriah Church in 1934, his first and only pastorate. An eloquent speaker in both English and Welsh, and a much loved and respected man, he worked industrially and unselfishly in the interests of his congregation and beyond. Mr Bowen was conductor of the Welsh National Eisteddfod for ten years during which time he also served as a member of the Eisteddfod Council. He then went on to be the president of the Eisteddfod drama and elocution section before, in 1956, being initiated as a member of the Gorsedd of Bards at Llangefni Eisteddfod. Mr Bowen was keenly interested in youth work in Rhymney, the Welsh organisations in the town, and in particular supported the Educational Settlement organisation in the Rhymney Valley. A major contribution to Welsh education in Rhymney was his support, in 1951, for Saturday morning Welsh nursery classes, initiated, on a voluntary basis, by interested parents who took 2 to 3 year-olds into their homes to familiarise them with the Welsh language. Beginning in a modest way with singing and recitals, numbers soon grew big enough for a formal move to be made to nursery classes in the vestry of Seion Chapel to be followed by the Tabernacle Chapel vestry in what was to be called The Welsh Nursery School (Ysgol Feithren). The Boys' Club premises at Tan y llan were at a later date also used for this purpose. With the support of such notables as the Rev. Rhys Bowen, Rev. and Mrs Lloyd of Penuel Chapel, Idris Davies the poet, the Rev. A E Grant and Bob Roberts of Seion Chapel, together with local Welsh teachers and interested enthusiastic townspeople, the education in Welsh of older children also grew in strength. From 1951 to 1955 Saturday morning voluntary classes were held in the Upper Rhymney Infants School and this was followed by the opening of the Rhymney Welsh School in Middle Rhymney Infants School in 1955.

138. Above we see Nanci Jones receiving an award for her loyal 25 years service to Welsh nursery schooling in the town. With her, from left to right, are to be seen schoolteachers Miss Hyde and Dilys Williams, husband Griff Jones, daughter Cynthia, Nanci, teacher Ceinwen Williams, presenter Nelly Morgan, Mair Young, teacher Heulwen Williams, Ann (Cunningham) and Shirley Evans.

On the night of 14th May 1940 the Secretary of State for War, Anthony Eden, broadcast an appeal to the nation that was to stir the hearts of everyone in all the cities, towns, villages and hamlets throughout the country. The country was at war, the perilous 'Miracle of Dunkirk' was desperately taking place and invasion appeared imminent by German troops. The Regular Army was engaged in a life and death struggle with the enemy. Arms, transport and equipment had been abandoned on beaches and battlefields along the line of retreat and the country was in serious danger. In the interests of national safety a line of defence had to be produced that would give the Regular Army breathing space in which to re-arm, re-equip and re-organise itself. Thus was born the LDV, local defence volunteers who responded immediately to the Minister's appeal by enthusiastically giving all their time in the interest of the security of the country. Overnight a peoples' army was born whose role was, in the probable event of an invasion by air, to watch, report, shadow, and if possible harass the enemy from the moment of landing. Initially organised in town groups and wearing arm-bands the LDV were responsible for providing their own arms which, in most cases, consisted of knives, clubs, rusty shotguns, pick-handles and ancient revolvers, often without bullets. The very small number of rifles that was available for issue were provided with five rounds of ammunition each. In Rhymney the Recruitment Office and Headquarters of the local defence volunteers was set up at the brewery under the command of Colonel J D Griffiths, backed by his second-in-command Lieutenant-Colonel Hoare. Housed in the drawing office of the brewery it was considered one of the better quality HQs when compared to others that might be located in Drill Halls, Police Stations or even garden sheds. So well did it serve the needs of the peoples' army it was subsequently adopted as the Battalion Headquarters with, initially, five Companies covering as far south as Pengam in the Rhymney Valley and eastwards as far as Markham in the Sirhowy Valley. The Rhymney, Rhymney Bridge and Abertysswg districts eventually became 'A' Company of the 6th Monmouthshire Battalion Home Guard, consisting of 650 members, and its establishment rung the death knell on its enterprising predecessor, the LDV.

139. Here we see some of the HQ staff of the 6th Battalion, the West Mon Section, who were housed in the brewery during the war years. Almost all brewery employees, they additionally worked night and day in the map-filled drawing office of the Estates Department taking signalled messages and co-ordinating the activities of the Companies within the field. Training was given in telephone duties and morse code and practice in fire drills with stirrup pumps undertaken at the nearby brickyard. In our photograph are to be seen, from top left, Joan (White) Howells, Olga Blake, Edwina (Price) Llewellyn and Elizabeth Williams. In the middle row are Myra (Richards) Williams, Rene Webber, Eleonor Jones and sister Gladys Jones, Mary Hannah (Edwards) Lance, Morfydd Jones and Minnie Jones. In the front row are Beryl Jenkins, Norma Kedward, Brewery Chairman Lt-Col G L Hoare, Col A J D Griffiths, Capt Maund, Ray Thomas and Ivy Rawle.

The Home Guard, now a co-ordinated force and an integral part of the British Army, was equipped with uniforms and arms brought to the Brewery HQ by brewery lorry from the Monmouthshire TA Depot. These were delivered to the Quartermaster, a Mr Bassett, and allocated to the Company Commanders by Captain Gallop who acted as both Sector and Battalion Adjutant.

140. Here we have a Rhymney contingent of 'A' Company, now fully uniformed and rid of their magical LDV arm-bands, among whom are to be seen Harry Breen of Hill Street, Tom 'The Shop', grocer, of Queen's Square and Billy Goode of Forge Street. These were the men who were responsible for road blocks throughout the town, checking identity cards, manning pill boxes and assisting in rescue work. Their exploits were sometimes serious, sometimes hilarious. The Battalion's first major alarm was on a hot Sunday in June 1940 when it was reported that five or six parachutists had been seen dropping on the Fochriw mountain. Colonel Hoare was immediately woken from his afternoon nap and he proceeded to the local police station to receive whatever information was available on the landing. The Sergeant-in-Charge, however, had already bravely made his way, single-handed, up the Fochriw mountain with half the weapons of the neighbourhood, one rifle. Colonel Hoare then set about commandeering all passing cars and arranged for six brewery lorries to block the roads on the High Street to Rhymney Bridge and at Penuel Row. Everyone at large was stopped and their identity cards examined and LDV volunteers mustered at Albion Square in readiness, armed with large knives or any other lethal weapons that they could lay their hands on. Hoare then went again to check his defences at Penuel Row and Rhymney Bridge and in an outlying defence post at the Rhymney Water Works. Satisfied with their invincibility he then returned to his troops at Albion Square to await events. In the meanwhile a message had got through that the women of Pontlottyn had gone up to the Fochriw mountain armed with knives for a head-on assault. The Battle of Albion Square, however, was destined never to reach the columns of the military archives for, what had been seen as invading German parachutists were, in fact, just five back-fires from one of our own passing aeroplanes.

| Gas Mask | Protection of your Home etc. | Stirrup Pump |

141. Here are the officers of 'A' Company who drilled, inspected, trained and supervised the activities of the local Home Guard unit among whom are to be seen Teddy Gower, Pete Shepherd, Harry Breen, Jones 'Cloth Hall', Harold Burnell and Eddie Williams. As sophistication grew in the local force, what started off as a temporary measure to combat any landing of enemy troops in the area developed into a far more wider context. The LDV, and then the Home Guard, would soon be called upon to guard vulnerable points, to protect industrial undertakings such as pits, works and reservoirs, to undertake counter-sabotage work, to identify Fifth Column activities and to co-operate with and assist the Civil Defence and the Police in the course of their duties. Still only a voluntary, part-time force, the Home Guard continued to need training in operational duties and in the new ideas, weapons and tactics that were evolving. An amusing tale surrounds the introduction and testing of a new innovation known as 'The Hedge Hopper'. Hedge Hoppers were large steel drums containing approximately forty gallons of inflammable material which were hidden behind walls and hedges and propelled at passing unfriendly tanks or fighting vehicles, exploding on impact. Colonel Hoare and Captain Gallop decided, however, that these were too big and cumbersome, and that five-gallon containers were more easily transported and could do the job just as effectively. They therefore set about making a number of smaller Hedge Hoppers which were to be tested before a galaxy of high-ranking officers to be specially brought in for the occasion. On the day the stage was set and Sergeant-Major Evans sat poised behind a canvas screen with hedge-hopper and propulsive charges at the ready, awaiting the signal. The signal was given but, of course, something went seriously amiss. There was an ear-splitting roar and the barrel hopped, and hopped, and hopped, and was never seen again! And, to cap it all, before the assembly could recover from its shock, they were descended upon and attacked by swarms of angry insects. They filled the air, maddened by this intrusion into their breeding ground, and chased the spectators as they fled the mountainside, to the accompaniment of much hand-clapping and waving.

*in a raid_*

Do not rush, take cover
quietly, then others will
do the same.

142. 'A Family at War', members of the Andrewartha family show pride in their contribution to the war effort as they come together in 1941 for this photograph. Standing, from left to right, are the young Neville Andrewartha, then Eric Andrewartha, Ron Kilby, Betty Kilby and Kenneth Andrewartha. Seated, all Andrewarthas, are Bill, Albert, Gladys (nee Moore) and Violet. Civil Defence groups were trained during the war to deal with every possible eventuality and, besides the Home Guard, the police force and the fire service, there were air-raid wardens, firewatchers and communication personnel. They were taught how to handle incendiary bombs, gas attacks and even the worst scenario, the aftermath of an air-raid. Air-raid wardens patrolled the streets to ensure that windows were blacked out, blowing their whistles loudly to ensure that everyone had heard an alert warning, and ringing their bells following an all clear. Car headlamps were masked, allowing only a horizontal split of light to be revealed. Windows were taped or papered against bomb blasts and doors made gas proof with tape or rugs.

143. The Headquarters of the Rhymney ARP group was in the Queen's Hotel and aside we see three of the Andrewartha family, Beattie, Betty and Gladys, two of whom are dressed in their ARP uniforms, in the yard of the hotel. Identified by the bold 'W' on their helmets ARP members wore the protective clothing shown and carried their first aid kits slung in a bag over their shoulder.

144. Rhymney, in common with many other towns in the valley, played its part in giving refuge to fleeing Belgians during the First World War. Germany's invasion of Belgium in 1914 created a tremendous feeling of outrage throughout the country and was a major reason why Britain entered the war. About a million refugees fled Belgium and by the end of 1914 nearly 200,000 had arrived in the country, destitute and in a state of shock, having seen their families killed and homes burned. The 7th of September 1914 saw the first contingency of refugees arrive in the Principality at the Cardiff distribution centre where the Lord Mayor, Dr James Robinson, had formed a refugee committee. In Rhymney, Noddfa House was one place of refuge where Belgian families were housed and supported by government grants and charity funds. The secretary of the committee which looked after the refugees in Rhymney was Tom Jones of 100 High Street. A group of the refugees is shown above and, third from the right, is Adeline Felicite 'Andree' Guillaume, who is seen with friends and relatives at Noddfa House. After the war Andree remained in Rhymney and went on to marry Bernard Wilfred Blake, an underground repairer who lived in Harcourt Terrace. She was never again to see her three brothers who remained in Belgium, one a silversmith and another a brigadier general in the Belgian Army. For a number of years Andree helped out in the snooker hall of the Workmen's Institute on Surgery Hill. Their daughter, Olga Blake, now Pearson, worked in the brewery for many years where, during the Second World War, she worked in the offices of the Home Guard unit.

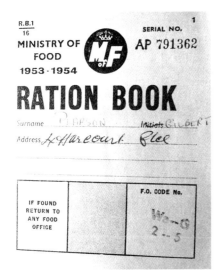

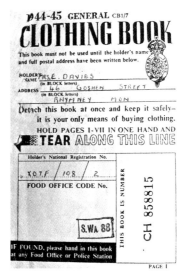

145/146. Examples of a Ration Book and Clothing Book that were in use during and after World War II. Because of the scarcity of food, rationing continued for many years after the war when it was normal for individuals to receive perhaps only one egg, 2oz. of bacon or meat and 1oz. of butter and cheese each week to supplement a diet of bread, potatoes and greens. Families would often have to walk miles and queue for hours for the most basic of needs but, however depressing it was, people supported each other and made the most of what they had.

147. Rhymney Cottage Hospital in 1939 during the war years is shown suitably sand-bagged and fronted by some senior staff and hospital board managers at a presentation event. Among the group from left to right are to be seen Gomer Jones, Enoch Jones, Evan Pugh, the hospital matron, Mrs Berry presenting Dr 'Bob' Redwood with a cheque, Dr Vernon Jones (it is believed) standing between two sisters, local bank manager Tom Harrison, David Thomas and William Evans. Dr Robert 'Bob' V De Acton Redwood served the hospital for 42 years until his death in 1947. To show appreciation for his work, the hospital was renamed The Redwood Memorial Hospital and a commemorative plaque was placed on the outside wall of the building near the main entrance.

148. Clearly enjoying the occasion we see some well known faces at the annually held Hospital Ball in the mid-1950s. Among those in the front row are to be seen Archie Griffiths, Council Chairman Roger Williams, and local police sergeant Bob Jones. Elsewhere can be seen Malcolm Jones, Hilary Ogbourne, Connie Lloyd, Roy Watkins, Ray Hapgood, Sergeant Tom O'Connell, Matron Roberts, Gwen Parfitt and Mary Francis with husband Miles.

149. The enthusiasm and hard work of a small caring group of Rhymney ladies has, for many years, helped bring comfort, pleasure and support to hundreds of disabled and needy folk in and beyond the town. The driving force that inspired Pauline Hatton of Moriah Street to found the Hafod Deg Junior Support Group in 1979, with the enthusiastic support of the children of Rhymney, has to date provided over £30,000 of funding to charities and handicapped centres in the area. Starting off in a small way with Pauline as its founder and competent producer, Janice Rees as its pianist, Irene Savage as its treasurer and with the help of Beverley Davies during its first year, the group's aim was to purchase a minibus for the benefit of the Hafod Deg Centre for the Handicapped and other centres in the area. Fund-raising was to be accomplished through the efforts of a committed troupe of children who would, under Pauline's direction, produce pantomimes and variety shows and provide evenings of entertainment at local centres for the handicapped. With ready support from local organisations and through their fund-raising activities the minibus was proudly purchased nine months later.

To widen their scope the successful group's name was changed to the Young Generation in 1981 and it continued to grow to provide money for equipment for various centres, to fund day trips and entertainment, and to respond to various appeals nationally as well as locally. Some organisations that have benefited from their hard work have been the Oakland Handicapped Centre, the Prince Charles Hospital Heart Appeal, Velindre Hospital, the Aid for Deaf Children Appeal, the MacMillan Nursing Appeal Fund, Helping Hands, the Jayne Hodge Home for Children, the Chernobyl Childrens Appeal Fund, the Tredegar Hospice of the Marches and the Hafod Deg Centre.

The Young Generation, a voluntary and non-profitmaking group, continue in their spare time to enthusiastically bring pleasure to the needy and their musical skills have also been applied to, and borne fruit from, many competitions over the years. In 1981 the group entered the Rhymney Eisteddfod and gained first prizes in two age categories of the Action Song competition and took two first prizes in solo competitions. A later eisteddfod entry brought further successes with first, second and third prizes in action and solo events. In appreciation of the fine work undertaken by this caring band of troupers and their competent producer, Whitbread Wales presented them with a Community Award in 1984 which was presented to them at the Rhymney Comprehensive School by its then headmaster Gwilym Lewis.

The above photograph shows the Young Generation of 1996 with pianist Janice Rees and producer Pauline Hatton. In the back row, from the left, are Elizabeth Squires, Emma Cooper, Christopher Squires, Greg White, Ian Pearce and Bethan White. Next row down can be seen Gemma Brooks, Greg Plant, Matthew Brown, Christopher Morgan, Adam Cooper, Matthew Diggle and Tracey Walters. Then, below, are Andrea Lang, Natalie Powell, Ceris White, Angharad Williams, Elizabeth Diggle, pianist Janice Rees with Alexandria Lewis on her knee, producer Pauline Hatton holding young Abbe Davies, Sian Lewis, Carli Watkins and Lisa Watkins. Fourth row from the top are to be seen Rachel Morgan, Claire Harris, Angharad Probert, Clare Lewis, Ceri Ann Jenkins, Kylie Davies, Nicola Charles, Charleen Evans, Jayne Bishop and Sarah Carter. Finally in the front row are Natasha Davies, Ceris Harris, Abbe Brown, Rebecca Davies, Stephanie Edwards, Zoe Savage, Jessica Lewis, Victoria Jones and Krystina Norris. The treasurer of the Young Generation is Irene Savage.

150. Some of the professional and business people of Rhymney in 1940 who were members of the '20-Club'. Standing, from the left, are Vic Lewis, I Thomas, Idris Davies, Ivor Glencross, H Moseley, W Davies (post office manager), Mr Edwards, D Thomas 'Cymro', Tom Harrison (bank manager), R Cox, Dr Ieuan Evans, A Matthews and T Jones. Seated are Freddie Maddocks, D A Moseley, G Fisher, Jones 'Cloth Hall' and Teddy Glencross.

151. A company of James Smith employees present their concert of gypsies in 1952. Thanks to the memory of Iris Vaughan, from top left are to be seen Anne Jane Brown, Madge Morgan, Nellie Perkins, Glenys Bromage, Nellie Hart, Katie Williams, Megan Matthews, Hatty Williams, Edie Goode, Tony Cusack, Bill Watkins, Gwladys Evans, Polly James, Cassie Gardner and Edie Pearce. In front, from left to right, are Mair Davies, Mary Lewis, Jean Woods, Mair Breeze, Hetty Maunders, Betty Lewis, Joan Rowlands, Winnie Morgan, Vera Breeze, Ann Williams and Ira Davies.

Tom Idris
"Doh Ray Me"
Davies

Popeye
James

Weeping
Willie

Twm
the warmed up
corpse

Dai "Central `eating"

Billy
Sniff-Sniff

Dai
Moustache

152. With so many people bearing similar surnames such as Davies, Jones, Evans, Williams, Morgan and so on it is no wonder that they needed to be identified by their own, often very personalised, nicknames. Tom Jones could be one of many but Tom 'The Laundry' was immediately recognisable, as was Tommy 'Aberystwyth', Tom Jones 'Ty Cwtch' and Tom Jones 'Number 5', who happened to grow up to become Dr Tom Jones 'Cabinet' but who, in his classroom, was simply a number among the many Tom Jones's in his class. But what was probably once a necessity was soon to develop into a philosophy, almost a way of life, when practically everyone had to be given a nickname, for humorous if not for practical purposes. So were invented a huge range of appellations, some funny, some insulting, some rude, but all having a bearing on an idiosyncracy of the nominee, where he came from, what his occupation was or what he looked like. From North Wales came the 'Gogglers', from Carmarthen the 'Sir Gaers'. More locally there was May 'The Glwyd' who lived by the Butetown toll-gate, Gerry 'Bryn Oer', Jim 'Nant y Melyn' Williams, Elvet 'The Ras', Mrs Powell 'Old Furnace', Megan 'Brickyard House', Myfanwy 'Ty Isha', Gwyneth 'Twyn yr Arian', Ollie 'Penrheol', Willie Thomas 'Llangorse' and John Owen 'Rock' who played the concertina at the local penny readings. Occupations provided a useful means of identity and particularly cryptic was Davies 'The Death Club' who collected life insurance premiums. Then there was Danny 'Cappo' the carpenter, Rees 'Queen' who kept the Queen's Hotel, Jones 'Cloth Hall' who ran a men's outfitters on the High Street, Jones 'The Wheelwright' with his workshop in the Cutting, Ivor 'Milgi' who bred greyhounds, Dai 'The Post' Williams, bakers Joe 'Bacws' and Albert 'Y Bara', Harry 'Ceilog' Williams who kept chickens, Nat Harris 'Pen Steps' whose shop was situated above a flight of steps on Queen's Square and Jenkins 'The Oil' who travelled the villages with his horse and cart selling domestic oil. Physical peculiarities evoked some hilarious, but often cruel, nicknames and the author has no intention of upsetting anyone from those that are recorded. One for the history books must surely be Dai 'Central eating' who had but one solitary tooth remaining in his upper gum! Then there was Billy 'Six Months' who, on one side, had but half a ear. Danny 'Bach' Owen was small in stature, as were schoolteachers Billy 'Nip' and Daniel 'Mishtir Bach' Thomas. Harry 'Cochyn' had red hair and Eddie 'Tondu' Williams had black. Dai 'Double Yolk' was the proud father of twins and Johnny 'Look at the Moon', of Brynteg Crescent, was forever inviting people to look skywards. There was Tom Idris 'Doh Ray Me' Davies who was always chanting his tonic solfa and Marie 'Cloggy' who always smelled strongly of cologne. One that cannot be overlooked is High Street cobbler 'Cachu Sprigs' who held small quantities of sprigs in his mouth while tapping shoes, occasionally swallowing one or two, but ridding himself of them by allowing Mother Nature to take her natural course. Many hundreds more could be added such as Tommy 'Tut Tut', Morris 'Yankee', Jones 'Dinah', Johnnie 'Fresh Air', Will 'Puss Puss', Maggie Jane 'Faggots', Harry 'Kong', Billy 'Oy Oy' Lloyd, Tommy 'Put me Tidy' and Lizzie 'India China'. The list is endless but I am afraid that space is limited.

153. Rhymney Youth Band originated in 1949 under John Price of Hill Street, using recorders loaned by the Monmouthshire County Council and they first of all practised upstairs in the Company Shop at the bottom of Surgery Hill. The idea of a band was conceived by two old bandsmen, Idris Jones and George Crompton while working at their jobs on a building site in Newport. Anxious that Rhymney should have a band again they set about to rent a room in the Workmen's Library for 2/6d (12½p) to hold a meeting in order that discussions might be initiated on the possibility. With support from local councillors the idea became a reality and posters were displayed throughout Rhymney in order to recruit suitably interested youngsters. And so was born the Rhymney Youth Band which, without instruments or uniforms, was taught the basics of beat and timing by John Price, and practised on their recorders in anticipation of one day becoming a Silver Band. Enthusiasm was high, both with band members and with the local council and miners' welfare committee, and, thanks to substantial grants and generous support from the public, enough money was raised in 1950 to provide the band with a full set of instruments. An impressive ceremony was held in the town to mark the occasion and a service of dedication was given by Canon Cooper Lewis.

An earlier Rhymney Youth Band, shown above, played under the conductorship of Richard Nash who was to be involved with brass bands for over 65 years. The group consisted of, from top left, Vic Davies, Gareth Richards, Gerald Harris, David Buckley, Olwen Davies, Brian Roberts, Wynne Thomas, Philip Davies and John House. Below are to be seen Nigel Mumford, Jimmy Price, Leslie Weaver, Dilys Mumford, Ann Roberts, Glyn Meredith, Michael Hancock, Estelle Gower, George Crompton and David Richards. In front are Trevor Mumford, Byron Trowbridge, Elaine Crompton, Danny Lloyd, conductor Richard Nash, Teddy Gower and Ron Davies.

154. The superb photograph on the previous page of the 1915 Rhymney Brass Band was taken in front of the corner of Jenkins Row, below the lower park gates, at a time when street lamps were lit by gas. The name of each bandsman is shown with, no doubt, the dignitaries and officials standing behind and the children sitting in front, taking great pride in their display. Brass bands in Rhymney go back as far as the 1830s when, not only one, but as many as three or four bands would be seen on a Saturday evening temperance procession marching through the town or over the mountain from Rhymney Bridge to Dowlais Top. The pledged abstainers would carry multicoloured Japanese lanterns in their hands and would march along, as darkness fell, like a snake of light, heartily singing their militant temperance songs. One of the best bands was led by Gwilym Gwent (William Aubrey Williams, 1834 - 1891) or Bilo Bach as he was known. Gwilym was a short, jovial, unassuming blacksmith who smoked a clay pipe and spoke only of music and musicians. He composed anthems, songs and band pieces completely in his head before committing them to paper and his best remembered piece is 'Yr Haf', a tribute to summer which he wrote in Cwm Mawr in Blaen Rhymni. Many enthusiasts followed in Gwilym Gwent's footsteps to sustain the tradition of bands in the town.

155. Between the war years was seen another chapter in the history of Rhymney which was to bring further suffering and pain to her families, the general strike and lockout of 1926. It was a time that required the mining population to rally round and pull together in the interests of their self-preservation, and this they did with dignity and pride. The town, along with all those in the South Wales coalfield, was a town of colliers which meant that practically all the working force was in some way affected by the closure of the pits. Innovation was stretched to the limit to provide food for the table; potatoes mixed with flour by bakers and at home would help increase the size of loaves and dandelion roots were chopped up and used as a coffee substitute. Allotments were put to their optimum use and local farmers and shopkeepers gave what they could to help relieve the widespread starvation. And so were born the soup kitchens which sprang up in many chapel vestries, schools and public buildings throughout the town. Our photograph above shows the men who helped run the Rhymney Urban District Council Distress Committee soup kitchen, believed to be a group from a lodge of workers' union officials. These men, among whom are Ned Lewis, Tim Greaney and Parry Jones, would have collected food, fresh and left-over, from a hundred and one sources to maintain a huge stewing cauldron of broth continually kept on the boil from which to feed a hungry population. The broth would contain anything available that would provide sustenance and included such things as potato and swede peelings, cereals of all sorts, butter and fat, bones, lentils, anything in fact that was not sweet by nature or of the cabbage family. Beyond the soup kitchens people did all they could to raise money for food. Entertainment committees were set up and jazz and gazoota bands, penny reading concerts, social evenings and various tournaments were arranged to help provide funds.

156. Although the 1926 strike was called off unconditionally after nine days, the miners still carried on their long drawn-out struggle to improve their working conditions and those who refused to work for lower wages were locked out of the pits. Much sympathy was shown by certain sectors throughout the country for the miners' plight and collections were frequently being made at railway stations and high streets to send to the Welsh coalfield. Makeshift choirs organised themselves on marches through neighbouring English counties to sing and beg for money, goods or food.

Above we see the Penuel Chapel soup-kitchen members in 1927 in the chapel grounds with the Upper Rhymney Infants School behind. Some names have been provided by Rene (Matthews) Jones who remembers among the group Isaac David Rees, Thomas 'Tom R' Richards, Mrs Bryn Roberts, George Lewis (Goshen Street), Jim Matthews (Cambrian Street), Mr and Mrs Acreman (Cambrian Street), Anna and Margaretta Matthews, Jones 'Ty Cwtch' and Mrs Davies.

157. Coal-picking from the 'patches' provided heating for the home and a certain amount of income for destitute families and men, women and children would be seen, often under cover of darkness, filling sacks of coal but, at the same time, keeping a sharp look-out for the local 'bobby'. To help married men with families a Miners' Welfare Grant was payable to those who would work on the construction of new roads and houses. Such a group of unemployed from Rhymney is shown above working on a road building scheme at Caerwent in 1926. Many other families, a quarter of a million in total in South Wales, emigrated to countries such as Australia and Canada during this period to escape the poverty.

158. Rhymney Post Office as it may be remembered in the fifties with postmaster Will Davies nursing his child outside. It was a time when mail was delivered on foot whether down an icy, wintry Surgery Hill or to an isolated farm on Blaen Rhymney. Every day and in all weather saw the spirited postman doggedly making his way to every corner of the town, sometimes pushing handcarts such as the one shown above, often being snowballed by school children when the snow was down. Some familiar faces over the years are shown below, together with their periods of service with the Rhymney Post Office.

159. Wilfred Evans 1913 to 1960

160. John Newton 1952 to 1995

161. Tudor Evans 1961 to 1989

162. Dai Williams 1937 to 1974

163. Rhymney's Red Cross Junior Link group was enthuiastically set up in 1976 under Link patron Elvira Lyons and had 61 members between the ages of eight and thirteen, trained by Red Cross nurse Valerie Davies. The Juniors arranged house to house collections in support of the Red Cross, organised jumble sales, entertained old people and handed out parcels to the disabled. Some Link members seen above are Emma White, Alan White, Clair James, Mandy Jones, Gail Worgan, Mandy Lawrence, Katherine Jones, Alison Jones, Louise Lyons, Steven Twigg, Edward Lawrence, Erica Oakley, Alison Holland, Sandra Edwards, Andrea Williams and Clair Jones. The photograph, taken on the first anniversary of the group, was also the occasion when fifteen new members were enrolled. The new members were Jacqueline Lawrence, Michelle Matthews, Piera Lewis, Natalie Jones, Diane Smith, Paula Jones, Linda Knight, Julie Weaver, Helen Price, Jason Kilby, Clair Buckley, Tracey Lewis, Mark Davies and Lisa Elliot. Adult Red Cross members to be seen include Gertrude Lawrence, Daphne Watkins, Norma Williams, Valerie Davies and Lena Jones.

Many of the children above also belonged to the original Young Generation group.

164. Rhymney over the years has made her mark in many corners of the world. On this occasion, 315 miles away at Lands End, a family group, not stranded we hope, continue to fly the flag. Clearly enjoying their holiday are Bill Jones, Brian Darlington, Lizzie Jane Breeze, Dilys Morgan, Alfie Morgan, Myra Davies and John 'Coffee' Davies.

165. Friendly Societies were self-help groups set up locally early in the 19th century, having gradually taken the place of the old medieval craft guilds. Often called benefit clubs they were voluntary organisations open to anyone who could pay the required contribution and their purpose was to provide a weekly relief to members who may have come upon hard times because of illness or injury and to give financial support to such things as burial costs. Local friendly societies were set up within the community by such groups as bricklayers, farmers, firemen, stonemasons, women, mechanics and even lovers of the Welsh language. They usually met twice a month, often in a public house, to discuss their business. Some, such as the Rhymney Bridge Friendly Society shown above, were locally organised and autonomous while others were affiliated to a wider organisation such as The Ancient Order of Foresters, The Unity of Oddfellows, The Ancient Order of Shepherds and the Philanthropic Order of True Ivorites. The Ivorites, an order founded in 1836 and unrepresented beyond Wales, were particularly strong among the Welsh contingency in Rhymney and held their meetings in the Castle Hotel. A strict society, its members were fined during meetings for 'intoxication, sleeping during proceedings, swearing, singing an indecent or political song or for 'speaking in an offensive tone or sentiment'. Such societies provided help to its members when most needed and the inhumanity of The Poor Law in 1834 drove many to join for the protection that they gave. A well-known Ivorite, poet David Evans (Dewi ap Shon), a faithful member of Seion Chapel, was buried with full Ivorite honours in Graig cemetery. He did much in his life to locally support the Ivorite policies of promoting the Welsh language and literature within the town.

The Rhymney Bridge Friendly Society shown here in 1919 held their meetings fortnightly in the Rhymney Inn (Beaufort Arms) and, thanks to the remarkable memory of Gwyneira Williams, formerly of Cambrian street, we are able to provide some names. In the back, from left to right, can be seen Fred Price, Polly Moseley, unknown, Nathaniel Williams, John Henry Williams, Mary Elizabeth Price, Sarah Williams, Mr and Mrs Magness, Martha Williams, two unknown, D Williams, Rhys Williams from Brecon and Mr Davies from Top House, Graig Row. In the middle row can be seen Daniel Williams, Joe Price and wife, two unknowns, Mary Ann Williams, Sarah Davies of Top House, Graig Row, unknown, Gladys Benjamin, the organist of Graig Chapel, unknown, Polly Jones and Mr Williams. The only two identifiable in the front row are Harry Jones 'Benji' and Dewi Griffiths.

166. This is a gathering of Rechabites at a function held in the vestry of Jerusalem Chapel in the 1940s with Council Chairman David Thomas in attendance. Temperance societies, of which the Rechabites was one, were founded to foster abstinence from alchoholic drink. Rhymney and Pontlottyn, heavily populated in the early 1800s, was copiously provided with public houses, inns and hotels and the hard and heavy work, undertaken in hot conditions by the industrial community, demanded a ready supply of drink. Many lived in slum conditions and the local inn was a friendly place to congregate despite the inevitable drunkenness and brawling that ensued. Temperance societies were thereby set up by responsible and well-meaning members of the community, six branches in Rhymney, two for adults and four for the many children who were the victims of drink. Efforts were made, and much success gained, in promoting teetotalism and in reducing the number of public houses in the town but many grocers still refused to stop selling strong drink. The Rhymney branch of English teetotallers was known as The Lancaster Guns and The Irishmen of Gomorrah had their own successful group of abstainers in Pontlottyn.

Some faces from the above Rhymney Rechabite group have been identified as Lena Davies, Megan Hulbert and son, Dai Rich, Mr Edwards, Mr and Mrs Bill Pullman, Bessie Williams 'The Ras', Mrs Carey, Gladys Vaughan, Mrs Rosie Williams 'The Tips' and husband, Vaughan Edwards, Bronnie Edwards, Joseph Price, John Price, Tom Thomas, Olive Williams and Mr and Mrs David Thomas,

167. Members of Jerusalem Chapel Sunday School class in 1954 pose outside their place of worship. From the left are Eirwen Owen, Joan Williams, Maureen Morris, Enid Llewellyn, Pat Evans and Dwynwen Thomas.

168. The opening of the Rhymney Rugby Club in 1959 took place almost simultaneously with the switch to the Memorial Park ground and the erection of its grandstand. The newly built club was positioned where Andrewartha's greenhouse once stood behind the Royal Hotel. Prior to this the team had played at the Eisteddfod Field and changed at the Workingmen's Institute on Surgery Hill, the Workmen's Club on the High Street and in the Royal Hotel itself. The above photograph shows officers and guests attending the official opening, in 1953, of the new purpose-built pavilion at the Eisteddfod Field. The pavilion, which provided the luxury of hot showers, toilets and a rest room, was officially opened by Dai Jones (Blaina) of the Welsh Rugby Union. Some faces to be seen are John Protheroe, Joe 'Bacus' Williams, Maynard Brown, Dai Jones, Idwal Jones, A B Evans, Mr Lewis, Clerk to the Council, James Greene, Ron Cox, David Moseley, Norman Gilbert, Leslie Davies, Dai Rich and Council Chairman David Thomas.

169. Players of the Penydre football team relax at Tredegar outdoor swimming pool in 1948 in readiness for their next encounter. Standing, from the left, are Charlie Ward, Bryn Matthews, Billy Carroll, Ivor Price, Doug Simms and Lyndon Goode. Kneeling are Dick Price, Ron Price, George Simms and Berty Stevens.

170. St David's Church production of Philip King's *'Without the Prince'* was presented in 1951 under the direction of parish curate H R Hughson. Its cast, from the left, standing, were Tom Davies, Cissie Andrewartha, Norman Gilbert, Raymond Jones, Lucy Thomas and Tom Evans. In the front row are Muriel Henry, Ken Wilkins, H R Hughson, Mary Church.

171. Some well known faces from the Puddlers Arms enjoy a stop-off at Blackpool on their way to Murrayfield in support of the Welsh team against Scotland in 1955. In the back row, from left to right, are to be seen Mal Prosser, Billy Welsh, the hotel owner, John Davies, Griff Jones, Ted Phillips, Cyril Williams, John Williams, George Watkins, John Prosser, Eddie Jones and Billy Phillips. In the middle are James Spacey, Haydn Powell, John Morgan, Tommy James, Tom Ben Mumford, Viv Davies, Emlyn Powell, Will Probert and Will Smith. In front are seen Gwyn Parry, Ivor Bedford, Gwyn Mumford, Graham Crane and Billy Lewis.

172. A Rhymney Grammar School production, on this occasion, *'The Rivals'* in about 1952, demonstrating the huge amount of work that went into the manufacture of their costumes. The cast from left to right, standing, consisted of David Davies, Keith Hodges, Howard Smith, unrecognised, Alun Moseley, Tony Nash, John Bailey and Byron Trowbridge. Seated are Myfanwy Herriman, Desdemona Barnard, Janet Lodwick and Vera Horler.

173. Going back to 1927 here we have some of the older members of Jerusalem Chapel in the process of a concert production. Some names that may be identifiable are William John Narbed, Trevor Williams, William Griffiths, John Monk and Harry Davies.

CHAPTER 6
Princetown and Tafarnaubach

The village of Tafarnaubach, built around 1840, originally consisted of 53 dwelling places built on land owned by the Duke of Beaufort whose agent in 1917, a Mr Roberts, came from Llangynidr on horseback each week to collect the 6d (2½p) rent from tenants. Its homes were two up and two down, built with thick walls of sandstone and black mortar topped with slated roofs. In earlier days the village, together with Princetown, stood on the important east to west line of communication and felt the full impact of the travellers, drovers, and later the industrial traffic, that continually passed through the area. To cater for so much passing activity the villages were well provided with stopping places and as many as nine inns and beer-houses at one time existed there. With names such as The Swan Beer House, The Lamb Inn, The Twins Beer House, The Red Lion Beer House and The White Horse Inn, all now lost to the past, the villages would have buzzed with the comings and goings of ironstone workers, coalminers, brickyard workers, limestone hauliers and Irish navvies working in or passing through the area. From Trevil loaded trams of limestone were hauled by horse or limestone rock was carried in panniers by mule on a route behind the Travellers Rest, past Penbrith Farm and on to the Union blastfurnaces near Rhymney Bridge. Evan Thomas in 1858 ran his Taverni Bach Brickworks and Lime Kiln above White Horse cottages where he lived at Brickyard Cottage. Men from the village first of all worked in a drift mine opposite the Travellers Rest and many of them, in later years, shifted to Pochin Colliery on the arrival of deep mining. Joe James 'Y Gof', Tafarnaubach's blacksmith, busied himself shoeing horses, making metal hoops for cartwheels and tools such as chizels for local workmen, assisted by children to pump his furnace bellows. Census data also reveals a cordwainer at work in the village. A cordwainer was a shoemaker who worked in soft leather (derived from the word cordovan from a place called Cordova where it was originally used). Irish navvies, of course, worked for many years in the villages of Princetown and Tafarnaubach on the construction of the Bryn Oer tramway, its roads and on the Dowlais to Abergavenny railway line, and they added much to the colour and history of their time.

174. Penbrith Farm, from a painting by Idris Jones (The Ras), past which limestone was hauled from Trefil to the Rhymney blast furnaces. Nearby was the Brinbrith balance pit where iron ore was extensively extracted from the blue and red veins and which was closed in 1863. An underground horseway led from this pit to the Union blast furnace site near to what is now the Rhymney House Club.

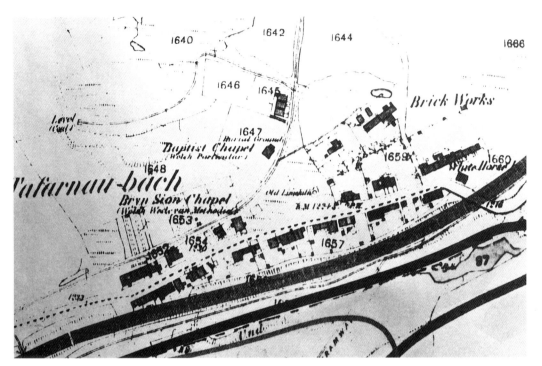

175. The early days of ironmaking saw much strife between the ironmasters and workmen and a busy Tafarnaubach experienced its fair share of the difficulties that ensued and the growth of the Chartists' movement. The 1830s was a particularly violent time between masters and men when wages were cut, housing facilities were appalling and the abusive Truck system was in force by the Company Shops. Children as young as five years of age worked in the mines, like their parents, from six in the morning to six in the evening, either as air-door boys or hauliers. With a solitary candle, cramped with cold and ill-fed, they would spend their lonely day, deprived of light and air, for a wage of a couple of pennies a day. A young twelve-year-old, Bill Humphreys, gave his impression of what children went through : 'I rest sometime in the mine to eat my bread and cheese, which is the only thing I take with me; we often lose our bread and cheese, the rats take it away; we are obliged to keep our candles in tin boxes or they will have them too'. Add to these appalling conditions the outbreak of cholera and the distress that it brought and it is not difficult to understand the desperation that gave birth to the 'Scotch Cattle' and the Chartists' rising.

On 18th April 1839 over a thousand people met at Bryn Bach at a Chartists' gathering to promote interest in the movement and to gain support among the public and in Parliament. This was a considerably more successful demonstration than had taken place a month earlier in the Star Field, Dukestown despite the presence of the famous eccentric and man of the people Dr John Price of Llantrisant.

At that time Chartists' meetings were being held far and wide and scarcely an evening went by without a spontaneous open-air gathering springing up somewhere. Speeches were called for, budding orators were allowed to give vent to their views and the singing of hymns and militant Chartists' songs ensured a steamy agenda. The atmosphere was euphoric and packed with enthusiasm for the cause with torch-light processions moving from one place to another. The road between Rhymney Bridge and Dowlais Top earned the name 'The Sacred Road' for the many processions that it bore. The overwhelming fervour reached a head in November 1839 with the ill-fated march to Newport when Charter supporters from the surrounding towns joined forces for a major demonstration at the Westgate Hotel. Three hundred people, many wearing the distinctive blue waistcoats and carrying pikes and rifles, marched past the Union Furnace at Rhymney Bridge, through Princetown and Tafarnaubach, to meet up with the Dukestown contingent led by Dai the Tinker. From here they went to Ebbw Vale to meet up with the Ebbw Vale, Beaufort, Brynmawr and Nantyglo demonstrators led by Zephaniah Williams, and then on to Newport. The shock and tragedy of the Newport confrontation,where nine were killed by waiting troops, saw the weakening of Chartism and within the decade its energies were assimilated by the growing trade union movement.

176. A flavour of Old Tafarnaubach is captured with this photograph of the Penybont area taken over forty years ago. Bridge Cottage, on the left, stood where the roundabout is now built and in the distance, looking over the bridge, can be seen Bryn Bach Farm in the area of what is now Bryn-Bach Park. Enjoying a day of festivity and suitably attired for the occasion are Olwen Watkins and Roy Jenkins.

177. Siloam Baptist Chapel, built in 1844, still stands today as a citadel to the hardworking miners and ironworkers who constructed it in an age of poverty, disease and uncertainty. Its congregation over the years had lived through the cholera epidemic and its cemetery bears witness to those who perished from its effects. Tucked away in a corner of the cemetery lie the remains of a small number of victims who were interred there before a new law introduced a ban on such burials and victims had, instead, to be buried in separate, specially prepared, burial grounds such as that at Cefn Golau. The Siloam group above, fortunately, saw happier times and among the smiling faces are to be seen Lloyd English, Paul Edwards, Hadyn Phillips, Margaret Chamberlain, Helen Jones, Barbara Chamberlain, Mair Jenkins, Mary Hannah Evans, Mary Arnold, Agnes Williams, Margaret Edwards, Peter English and Rhian English.

178. An historically cultural and exciting event at Bryn Bach in August 1990 was the arrival of the National Eisteddfod, which brought participants and spectators from all corners of the world. The climax of the event is shown above with the chairing of the bard Myrddin ap Daffyd of Capel Garman, Llanrwst Gwynedd. A well-known publisher, he founded Gwasg Carreg Gwalch in 1980. The Chair was carved by Ceri Vale of Caerphilly. Tafarnaubach, over the years has made its own prominent contribution to Welsh culture and not to he forgotten was Gwilym Tilsley who was successfully chaired at National Eisteddfods in Caerphilly and Anglesey and who then went on to become an Archdruid of the Gorsedd Circle. Tilsley, a young minister from Llanidloes came to preach at the Wesleyan Chapel of Bryn Seion in Tafarnaubach, living with the deacon of Siloam Chapel Dafydd Thomas and his good wife Margaret.

179. Another chairing took place in Tafarnaubach in 1953, this time of the coronation queen Marina Davies, during a national celebration day. Among her ladies-in-waiting can be seen Ann Harris, Glenys Saunders and Maureen Kelly.

180. The Twyn Hotspurs AFC was a representative team of the Bryn Seion Wesleyan Chapel, Tafarnaubach and gave a good account of themselves in the Tredegar and Ebbw Vale League, gaining many trophies in their name. They played on a pitch behind the Travellers Rest, 1,160 feet above sea level, in the hardest winter conditions imaginable, and were the idols of the schoolboys and villagers who supported them. Our photograph above of the 1923/24 Hotspurs team includes the following recognised players Dick Jones, T Watkins, Ebi Whale and David 'Seion House'.

181. Tafarnaubach once had its own rifle club and its badge, shown above, harks back to the days when the village played its part in the Home Guard within the Tredegar 'D' Company of the 6th Monmouthshire Battalion. M E Prosser of 4a White Horse Row served with the Company, winning a Defence Medal in 1941. The rifle club competed locally and on a County basis and their moment of glory was their success in winning the South Wales and Monmouthshire Challenge Shield in open competition. In the preliminary stages of this NRA shoot they achieved a commendable record score comprising the best of all possibilities, quite a major feat in itself. Members of that particular team included Lieutenent A Taylor, Corporal Walters, Sergeant Roberts and Private Hyde.

182. Children of Princetown (Rhymney Bridge) School pose proudly with headmaster Mr Neat in the late 1920s. In the back row, from left to right, are to be seen J Powell, I Hancock, T Trowe, I Harwood, B Watkins, A Leask, Roy Jones and W R James. In the middle row are P Williams, M Powell, Hannah Watkins, G Theophilus, I Price, H Griffiths, M Prosser and T Thomas. Sitting are C Moseley, G Jones, H Griffiths, M Woods, M Harwood, S Hancock, C Magness, R Thomas and H Davies.

183. Decked out in their fancy hats and about to enjoy their Whitsun tea party in 1951 is a group of the Siloam Chapel congregation. Standing, from left to right, can be seen Evan Owen, Roy Jenkins, Tom Price, Ken Bishop, Ieuan Davies, Roy Price and Ben Harwood. In the middle row are to be seen Jimmy Davies, unknown, Marina Davies, Ann Prosser, Marion Davies, Joanne Rowe and Vivian Vaughan, and in front Warren Williams, Heulwen Davies, Mary Knight, Eifron Jenkins, Mary Coombs, Jeffrey Davies, Beryl Harwood and Ivy Owen.

CHAPTER 7
Abertysswg

184. Dating back to the early 16th century Abertysswg Farm, situated alongside the Nant Tysswg stream (Blaen Nant Tussocke), was one of the earliest farms in the locality and as such experienced the considerable changes that have taken place in farming over the centuries. Its oak beams and panelled walls would have witnessed the clandestine meetings of priests and secret worshippers during years of religious intolerance. Its fabric would have rung with the songs and recitations of young Welsh voices when the first attempts at schooling were practiced there. A law in power from 1616 to 1633 enforced that all parishes were required to hold schooling facilities for their children and, in Cwm Tysswg, the farm provided such a 'circulating' school where children were made to bring a lump of peat every day to heat the schoolroom. Along with other farms, it would also have seen the effects of the cattle plague that swept through Wales in 1632.

Predominantly an upland sheep farm with its own meadow and associated 'coed-cae' for the wintering and lambing of its flocks it, over the years, would have additionally used oxen for hauling wagons, black cattle for calfing and mules and horses for draught work and riding. Sleds, called 'car llusg' were used in the fields for bringing in the harvest and of particular importance was the 'gwair man', a mixture of nutritious plants which were especially gathered for feeding to calves.

Sheep farming on local uplands goes back hundreds of years and was even taken up by Cistercian monks who settled in the area many centuries ago. The old Welsh breed of sheep were small and white-headed and these were crossed with Cheviots when introduced in the middle of the 19th century for their greater size and for the better wool that they produced. Cardigan sheep were also later introduced for their hardiness and greater suitability to the weather conditions. The damper and cooler weather conditions meant that sheep and cattle were susceptible to particular ailments that the farmer had to be alert to. Maggots in the fleece and skin brought by flies living in the ferns was quite common and wounds were cleaned out and oil applied. A lump of lard was used for sheep scouring and tea-grounds or saltpetre in clear water were given every morning to cure liver fluke. Cows suffering from constipation or blockage were dosed with hot beer and bran and footrot would be cured by cutting out the infected part and making the animal walk over burnt lime.

185. Cutting and harvesting the hay with the scythe took weeks with each cutter carrying his own sharpening tool or 'rip', an eight-inch long block of ashwood covered in grease and mixed-in sand. The hay was transferred from field to barn by a horse-pulled wagon called a 'gambo'. Wagons conformed to a local pattern and could usually be identified with the county in which they were made. Above is the typical Monmouthshire wagon which was widely used locally and which, in 1881, would have been in use by the Bowen family who were then at Abertysswg Farm. Records show that Evan Bowen, with his wife Sarah and son Evan (a 'scholar') farmed there at that date and with them lodged three waggoners Charles Davies, Jane Jones and a Mr George.

The area of Abertysswg, originally known as Abertowsowe or Abertowsowy in the time when the land was owned by Rolande Morgan in 1570, has over the centuries and through recent industrialisation, represented almost a microcosm of the history of South Wales coalfield towns. From a sparsely populated rural area of scattered farms with cottage industry and local market economy was evolved a community that was to live through the turmoil and tragedy of coalmining and ironmaking. Long gone is the time when grouse lived in the heather on the hills, when hare and rabbit abounded with fox and badger and partridges crept stealthily through the undergrowth. Rivers then held an abundance of trout and woodcock, snipe and curlew were to be seen in numbers. Landowners, who had the sole pleasure of the hunt, engaged keepers and bailiffs to strictly police and maintain their estates. Local farm tenants and their hands were paid as beaters during shoots and huge bags of hares and game would be taken from the land on a good day. The local farming population, although not allowed to take game, nevertheless enjoyed poaching rabbits and hares and trapping birds in the surrounding hills and woodland, although this was undertaken at great risk and they were severely dealt with if caught.

The Morgan family, later to elevate to the peerage as the Tredegars, continued to own the land at Abertysswg through the centuries, leasing part of it at the turn of the century to the Tredegar Iron and Coal Company. Thus industrialisation, with all its trauma, excitement, expectation and heartache was brought to the quiet hamlet of Cwm Tysswg and the official birth of the village of Abertysswg saw the light of day in 1897 with the sinking of No' 1 McLaren Colliery.

186. The coal industry and growth of the village was well established when the above photograph was taken and the 130 foot high iron-plate chimney stack of the McLaren Colliery is clearly seen belching its smoke across the valley. One of the additional benefits that the colliery brought to villagers was electricity, which was generated through a 250 volt dynamo at the pithead. The first coal was wound up from pit-bottom in October 1898, two trams per wind, and within twelve months production had reached the planned target of 750 tons a day. The first man to work the colliery was Daniel Davies and the first boy William Russell.

187. By 1902 the village was rapidly growing with 115 homes already built and with a population of 347. Houses were continually being constructed for miners, builders, quarrymen, roadmakers and labourers, businesses were being set up and Pwll Llaca Colliery, bought from the Rhymney Iron Company, had become one of the McLaren holdings.

Above we show an early view of Charles Street at a time of gas lamps in the street and with the typical load of coal on the roadside waiting to be carried through the house to the coal-shed in the back yard.

188. 1906 saw the sinking of No. 3 pit at McLaren Colliery, a hard and dangerous job for the nine men who were involved in it, but a boost to the community for the extra work that it brought. Sinking took place at a rate of five yards a week and by the end of January twelve yards of sinking had been completed by the Bargoed contractors W B Lloyd. By December of the same year the Big Seam vein had been reached at a depth of 256 yards, the Rhas Las seam at 296 yards by February 1907 and the Lower Four seam at 376 yards on the Farewell Rock floor in June 1907.

So much coal production required an efficient transport system and Abertysswg Station, near McLaren Colliery, saw its busiest years during this period. Viewed looking south towards New Tredegar the above photograph shows the single line to Rhymney which was worked by Electric Train Tablet. The curved line southwards from McLaren Colliery was double and had a rising gradient of 1 in 98 for its 5³/₄ miles to Aberbargoed.

189. Below Abertysswg coal production had been taking place at the Elliot Pits from as early as 1860, but the restlessness of the steep hillside towering above, the Moving Mountain, brought great unease to those within its vicinity. The mountain had moved five times since 1903 sending thousands of tons of rock to the valley floor below but it was in April 1930 that the greatest damage was done. It was then, on the twelfth of the month, that a vast avalanche of rock fell from the face of the mountain, overwhelming and ruining the offices and buildings of New Tredegar Colliery. A further avalanche followed smashing the main road from Abertysswg to New Tredegar and demolishing the railway line thereby completely cutting off communication from Abertysswg to Bedwellty. The colliery was never used again and the road and railway never reconstructed despite many appeals for a road link to be re-opened. The two railway stations at Abertysswg and Pwll Llaca were abandoned, the first later becoming a Pentecostal Chapel and the latter the home of the Curran family. The above photograph shows how New Tredegar Colliery and the surrounding area looked before the 1930 tragedy, with an earlier view of Troedrhiwfuwch in the background.

190. The welcome demise of Company Shop trading in Abertysswg, and its replacement by the innovative grocer Alfred Warn with his store at 3 Charles Street, had the effect of increasing free commerce in the village with other members of the community soon setting up businesses in their front rooms. The new Post Office, shown above, was run by post-master John Morgan, his wife and daughter Victoria. Another businessman was I R Clarke of 27, Arthur Street who, with the assistance of his daughter, set himself up as the village's first photographer in the 1920s.

191. This is the front of Williams the Railway shop at 5 The Green, another earlier trader in the village, when Oxo appeared to be very much the flavour of the day. Stan Williams is seen here with Mrs Tyler, her son, and Mrs Death. Also on The Green appeared the first bank in the village, a branch of Barclays run by David Davies in his front room converted to an office. Another 'parlour' bank was later opened at 6 Walter Street. The first Reading Room to come to Abertysswg was again in a front room in Charles Street and run by John Adams where two daily and two weekly newspapers were displayed for the public to read. Another was later opened in 3 Arthur Street in the charge of John Davies where four national dailies and three weeklies became available. Great strides were later made with the opening of 'The Shed', a tiny library, where a small selection of books, all fiction, were available on loan.

192. Time for relaxation for the colliery officials of McLaren Colliery as they enjoy an evening together in 1948. To be seen among the smiling faces of the officials Social and Educational Club, at their first ever dinner, can be seen President R W Tolfree, colliery manager; Chairman Robert Kendrick, Secretary George Greeves, Evan Price, Tom Mumford, Albert Barnard, Mike Pullen and Glyn Phillips. The Club was founded in 1947 with sixty members each paying one shilling (5p) a week and their aim, through lectures, instructional film shows and visits to places of interest, was to instruct and entertain members of the community.

193. Equally enjoying their evening are the ladies of the Abertysswg Workmen's Institute in 1970.

194.   Members of Abertysswg's Fire Brigade stand proudly to attention in 1929, immaculate in their appearance. Third from the right is Alfred Augustus Watkins of Arthur Street who gained a formidable reputation as a rope-splicer both in competition and in industry. Fred worked for the Tredegar Iron and Coal Company at Bedwellty Pits and McLaren Colliery for 56 years from the age of 13 until his retirement in 1946. For his extensive service with the fire service, 40 years in all, he was awarded a long service medal and bar. He was also a special constable with the National Fire Service and a member of the Lord Abergavenny Lodge of the RAOB. Following an honourable life in the service of his village Fred died in 1956 at 79 years of age and was interred at Dukestown cemetery.

195. Officials of the Abertysswg Workmen's Hospital receive a donation from colliery manager H Golding during a celebratory evening in the 1940s. From left to right are D E Kendrick, hospital committee secretary; Mr Jordan, chairman H Morgan receiving the cheque, M Price, Mr Golding, Miss Megan Roach, leader of the ladies' branch of the Labour Party and M J Williams.

196. Abertysswg nursing cadets in 1972 celebrate fifty years of tradition of St John's Ambulance Brigade in the village.

197. The McLaren and Ogilvie ambulance team proudly display their silverware, in keeping with the many years of success that the St John's Ambulance Brigade has enjoyed. This is the team that won the prestigious national championship in Blackpool in 1959 in addition to the divisional championship in Porthcawl in the same year.
Standing from left to right are colliery manager D J Lewis, undermanager G K Morris, Dr Bartram, R Edmonds, G Jones, W Skyrme, first aid officer and Sister J Perry. Seated are W Mail, F Bowen, team captain E Stockman, T Jones and T Williams. The trophies on display are the Area Silver Cup on the left, the National Mitchell-Hedges Silver Bowl in the centre and the Divisional Silver Bowl to the right.

CHAPTER 8

Pontlottyn

Since the 16th century, when earlier deeds referred to the area as Yn Ysglodyn, the village that is now Pontlottyn has seen much change over the years. From a forested valley floor, rich in flora and fauna, where oxen once pulled wagons and the sparse community lived a simple pastoral life, the hillsides, now bared to the elements, show the scars of the years between. Almost two centuries of heavy industrial growth brought the promise of riches to the thousands of workers who migrated here from other Welsh counties and from Ireland, Scotland and England, but few were to escape the poverty, hardships and tragedy with which they were confronted. The ironmasters and coal barons, on the other hand, profited hugely from their manipulation of men and materials and, having exhausted their resource, left with a fortune in their pockets.

198. One of the earlier developments in industrial Pontlottyn was Bute Terrace, shown above, but far earlier the Rock Inn, situated nearby, had enjoyed the years of pastoral peace that had gone before. Near to Rock Inn was built Rock Row, number one of which was a boarding house owned by Timothy Lynch where he lived with his wife and seven boarding labourers. Everyone, directly or indirectly, were in the employ of the Ironworks and Daniel Lynch, a puddler with the Company, lived in 1881 at number one Bute Terrace. In number two lived two labourers across from Ireland, Daniel Reagan and Daniel Harrington, both with their families and an Andrew Keef lived in number three. Pontlottyn at that time was dominated by Irish immigrants with smaller numbers of Scottish, English and Welsh people living among them, all in severely crowded conditions. A typical example was at number four Bute Terrace where Irishman Daniel Cronin, a boiler maker, lived with his family together with lodgers Thomas McKenny, a fireman from Scotland, Thomas Flemming who worked in the iron furnace and their domestic servant Mary McKenny. This was a typical pattern in workers' houses where a dozen or more would live and where sleeping space was at such a premium that a bed would be used by different families at different times of the day and night.

Tokens, Rock Inn, William Lewis Williams (Proprietor)

199. Overshadowed by the cinder tip behind, Pontlottyn in 1910, with horse and cart on the dirt road, and a solitary gas lamp in the Square, offered good quality shopping for those who could afford it. The India and China Tea Company, 'Cash Grocers', displayed its wares alongside Olivers the shoe shop, where the price of a pair of shoes ranged from 7/11d (40p) to 12/6d (62½p) and where pieces of leather could be bought for 2/11d (15p) to undertake ones own repairs. Yorks, straps which were wrapped around the ankles over trousers and boots to prevent coal dust, or even rats, from entering the trouser leg, could also be purchased there.

200. At the same time Joseph Thomas owned the general store shown aside, Mydrim Stores, in Union Street, where we see him, in 1909, with customers and his young assistant in the apron M H Davies.

113

201. The atmosphere of Old Pontlottyn is again brought to life with this photograph of Heol Evan Wynne Road taken in around 1920. In the background can be seen the ghostly remains of Pwll Uchaf Upper Pit where many Pontlottyn miners were employed since it was built by the Rhymney Iron Company in 1890 until its closure in 1912. The Pwll Uchaf shaft was 150 feet deep and worked The Yard coal seam and was fairly unique in the area in that it had a single oval-shaped bricked shaft. About 200 men and boys worked there and they filled an average of 600 small trams of coal for each 10-hour coaling shift. The second 10-hour shift was for repairing, packing and preparing the coal faces for the next day. Their record shift output was 720 trams, achieved by hand with mandrel, wedge and sledge. 25 ponies were used underground there and girls picked off coal in the screens.

In one of the small cottages of Heol Evan Wynne, with their tiny piece of ground and 'vainc' out front, traded the Jewish pawnbroker Tobias Fine who also had premises on 92 High Street, Rhymney.

202. Another photograph which shows the essence of the time is this 1907 still of High Street. Here, typically, we see a miner with his scarf crossed firmly across his chest and tucked into his pullover, a tightly wrapped baby being nursed in its shawl, young girls in white aprons and boots and a really gawdy piece of headwear being worn by the central lady.

203. The day of the Sunday School processions through town in some respects resembled an annual fashion parade with everyone making a special effort to turn out in their best clothes. The above parade in 1910 of local chapel congregations highlights the finery of the day, the millinery competitiveness between the ladies in their brightly decorated hats and the smart bowlers and straw boaters worn by the men. The Square lent itself ideally as an arena where the circular parade could progress or where ministers could preach and lead singing and prayers. The procession was accompanied by drum and fife and brass bands. The Church of England congregation of St Tyfaelogs was led by the vicar and made its way to Rhymney to meet up with its sister congregations there. They would then jointly walk, singing and playing music, to Nantllesg Vicarage to be provided at the gate with bread and butter, cakes and buns with a mug of tea, and there they would relax on the lawn, chat or play games on the nearby field.

204. A Pontlottyn drum and fife band that would have been in great demand to appear at parades, social events and in competition.

205. Blackpool was a mecca for trippers during the 1950s and coach-loads would descend each summer from the valleys' towns. In September 1956 the above Pontlottyn group of well-known faces are seen enjoying the sea air. Among them are to be seen Graham and Margaret Crane, Margaret Morgan, Mair Hall, Lillian Jones, Elsie 'Bibby' Jones, Hilda Morgan, Pat Greaney, Cassie Gronnad, Doris Taylor, Nellie Perkins, May Hall, Betty Evans and husband, Nancy Davies, Des Greaney, Peter and Lynne Morgan, Ivor Morgan, Malcolm Williams, Mary and Ron Bradley and Iris and Derek Evans.

206. A St Tyfaelog group gather with vicar J Hughes for a special occasion. Among the group can be seen Sheila Goch, Eira Jenkins, Pat Powell, Nancy Twmmy, Cliff Gardener, Mrs Greening, Mrs Gardner, Graham Jones and Mr and Mrs Ings.

207. The staff of Pontlottyn Junior School in 1941 consisted of, standing from left to right, Carey Thomas, Mr Howell, George Walters and Eben Morris. Seated are Ernest Browning, headmaster J P Isaac and T Jones. In front are W J Bloxham and D J Francis.

208. The school football team after, no doubt, another resounding victory, pose for the camera in 1968. Standing, from the left, are Jeff Roberts, Raymond Davies, Michael Davies, David Murphy, Howard Lewis and Bernard Tack. Seated are Clive Jones, Jeff Evans, Keith Davies, David Diggle, Jeff Morgan, Ieuan Prosser and Paul Bennett.

209. The Railway Inn, which occupied three of the eleven arches of the Pontlottyn viaduct, met its final demise in 1997 following 130 years of catering for the social needs of the community. Built in 1867 by local tradesman Mr Gwynne (known as Gwynne Bach) for a Miss Cesia Williams, it defied the wishes of the Rhymney Iron Company who were against its construction. The inn provided an important feature in the village, a curiosity, and a rare example of this type of building which was not structurally fixed to the stonework of the arches. At the time of its construction three other public houses also existed in the village, The Picton Hotel, built by George Evans in about 1814, The Nelson Hotel and the Blast Furnace Inn. The Blast was built in 1845 by Jenkin Edwards who was the manager of the Bute and Rhymney Blast Furnace. Originally his manager's house he converted the building to an inn and adopted the name of his old place of work.

210. Mums and their children of Pontlottyn attend an infants' welfare clinic in October 1951 which was held, again, at Bethel.

211. The Pontlottyn contingent of "A" Company of the 6th Battalion of the Home Guard, by now fitted out with uniforms and an integral part of the British Army, sported its own drum and bugle section. The civilians' army, initially consisting of local volunteers and known as the LDV, was established in May 1940 and had the immediate support of such organisations as the Powell Duffryn Company, local councils and Buchans Brewery without whose generosity it would have faltered from the start.

212. More defence workers of Pontlottyn, this time the air-raid wardens who, during the war, gave their time voluntarily in the interests of the community.

213. Edward Thomas Chapman was twenty years of age when he left Ogilvie Colliery to enlist in the Monmouthshire Regiment, with service number 4080657, in April 1940. He served with the regiment in North West Europe fighting for Normandy, Northern France, The Low Countries, at the Rhine Crossing and in North West Germany. In April 1945 his Company crossed the Dortmund-Els canal under orders to assault the thickly wooded ridge of the Teutoberger Wald which dominated the surrounding countryside. The ridge was strong defensively and guarded by a battalion of German officer cadets, all picked men and fanatical Nazis. Chapman, then a corporal, was advancing in single file with his section to be opened fire upon at short range, suffering heavy casualties. He immediately seized his Bren gun and, advancing alone and firing from the hip, he mowed the enemy down at point-blank range, forcing a withdrawal. His section was now isolated but Chapman doggedly refused to submit to further charges and grenade attacks and amazingly continued to repel and drive back the enemy. In the affray his Company Commander had been severely injured but Corporal Chapman went out alone to open ground, under withering fire, and carried his Commander the fifty yards to comparative safety. The officer unfortunately died from a further sniper's bullet which also wounded Chapman in the hip but, despite his injury, he refused to be evacuated and maintained his position with the Company until their position was restored. For his outstanding gallantry and superb courage Corporal Chapman was decorated with the Victoria Cross by H.M. King George VI at Buckingham Palace on 31st July 1945. He was released to the Royal Army Reserve in 1946 and went on to serve with the Monmouthshire Regiment of the Territorial Army until 1957 when he was discharged on termination of his engagement with the rank of Company Sergeant Major. For his services with the Territorial Army he was awarded the BEM in 1953. This amazing Pontlottyn man, who won one of the most coveted and supreme awards for valour in the field of battle, on return to civilian life went on to work at the Rhymney Engineering Company, as a porter on Pontlottyn station and then at ICI Fibres and British Nylon Spinners, Pontypool. He married his wife Rhoda Frances Jean Watkins of Belfast in 1942 and they have three children. The remarkable Corporal Chapman, VC., BEM., 1939-1945 Star, France and Germany Star, Defence Medal, British War Medal, Coronation Medal (1953) and Jubilee Medal (1977), presently living out his retirement in Cwmbran, continues to bring great pride to his home village of Pontlottyn.

CHAPTER 9

Fochriw

214. The above photograph shows the lower area of Penybanc with Cwmllwydrew Farm in the foreground and Penybanc Farm top right. Together with Llwyn Iago Farm (Fochriw Farm), they represent the oldest known stone-built farms in the area mostly built in the 16th century but with Llwyn Iago having been traced at least as far back as the 1420s. A previous, much older, settlement was excavated in 1938 by Eileen Fox, M.A., on the eastern side of the common in an area known as Graig Spyddyd above Ogilvie Colliery. At 1300 feet above sea level, and just above the tree-line, the settlement consisted of five or six homesteads irregularly spread over about one third of a mile. Understood to be of the 13th century the 'platform' houses, built into the hillside, were roughly constructed of stones and turf and were permanent settlements as opposed to the temporary 'hafods' which were for summer use only. Nearby excavations provided evidence of primitive iron smelting being undertaken on the hill by the settlers, probably using small bowl furnaces cut into hollows in the ground and called 'bloomeries'. Llwyn Iago Farm is thought to have been built on the site of what was originally a 'platform' house. The remains of Cwmllwydrew Farm now lie below the Darren Park lake while Penybanc Farm was abandoned in 1970 when it was condemned following an earth tremor. The area continues to be actively farmed, however, by the Chapman family since the 1960s and what were once the living quarters now serve as barns. The area of Penybanc was at one time a thriving community consisting of two rows of small houses, twenty-four in total, a school, a Pentecostal meeting place, Penybanc Farm, the Penybanc Hotel, a worker's cottage called Ty Mawr House and, at one time, an isolation hospital for smallpox victims. Nearby was a drift mine.

Exactly 350 years ago was fought the Battle of St Fagans which, at least for the time being, put an end to the Royalist cause in Wales. This was a time when King Charles and his Cavaliers were anxiously drumming up support in Wales and their route to Brecon was through Fochriw where they rampaged through the farms and cottages, hammering on doors and demanding allegiance to the King. It was a fearful time, especially as it was known that the opposing parliamentarian Cromwell and his Roundheads were strengthening for attack. The turmoil and panic created in the peaceful hamlet of Penybanc left such an impact that it is said the farms, some of which were 'safe houses' for Royalists, still ring with the shouts and bangs of the Cavalier ghosts as they rampage on their horses through the area. Glimpses, it is reported, are still occasionally seen of children, dressed in the costume of the 17th century, fleeing the terror that surrounded them.

215. This 1896 photograph of Fochriw Colliery indicates the extent of offices and surface buildings that the colliery contained during its period of coal production from 1863 to 1924. The colliery was owned by the Dowlais Iron Company and, as late as 1885, was still using open lights underground instead of the safety lamps that were prevalent elsewhere. The steam coal that was being mined 400 yards below the surface was particularly susceptible to fire damp but, despite an accident at Fochriw No 2 Pit and despite the many representations made, it was not until a much later date that safety lamps were installed. A further danger of Fochriw Colliery was that it was supplied by only one shaft, partitioned to provide upcast and downcast either side of the cage compartment. The foolhardiness of such a system was brought home forcibly in 1862 when the single shaft of Hartley Pit in the north of England was blocked, entombing 204 miners below ground. It took an Act of Parliament, following the disaster, to make it compulsory for all but the smallest mines to have two shafts.

216. This is how Fochriw looked a decade later in about 1905 with miners' cottages spread wide and waste tips surrounding them.

217. A time-encapsulating study of members of the Fochriw Miners' Institute around the turn of the century.

218. A decade later, in around 1916, saw the above pupils in the Top School under the watchful eye of schoolmistress Mary Ann Lewis 'shakes'. Among them are to be seen Clifford Davies, Hartwell Woods, Lizzie Mary Lawrence, Elsie Woods, Lucy 'Twm Twm' and Morfydd Hollister.

219. The Fochriw Ladies Choir of 1930 pose outside Fochriw School where they practised. Among them can be seen May Thomas, tenor Willie Davies, schoolmistress Betsy Ballard, Mary Jane Shankland, Iris Edwards, Elizabeth Ann Evans, Elspeth Lewis, Elsie Griffiths, Maggie Cumpstone and Cyril Cook.

220. The village's brass band prepares for competition on tour in 1921. With bandmaster Bill Powell can be seen Elwyn Lewis, Bob Rees, Hartwell Woods, Alcwyn Burrows, Stanley Rees, Albert Mantle, David Powell, Atwell Woods, Danny James and David John Price.

221. A throng of happy Fochriw trippers who will remember having stayed at the Roselea Hotel, Blackpool in 1964. To be seen are Louise Powell, John Mantle, Wendy Jones, Catherine Price, Ceri Williams, Ron Bradley, Malcolm Mantle, John Barnard, Gwyn Mantle, Margaret Banfield, Catherine Davies, Steve Jones, Rufus Dummett, Sheila Barnard, Gareth Evans, Mrs Charles Dummett, Ceridwen Dummett, Elsie 'Bibby' Jones, Colin Price, Annie Evans, Derlwyn Evans, Dolly Lewis, Mr and Mrs Banfield, Mary Bradley, Nancy Williams, Eirwen Evans, Ann Evans, Linda Bradley, Sharon Barnard, Corrinne Powell, Cyril Williams, Len Powell, George Dummett, Idris Williams, Margaret Williams, Florence Evans, Philip Evans, Des Evans,Hetty Evans and Will 'Pop'.

222. Same trip, same hotel but a different age group. The above youngsters, now no doubt approaching their forties, pose delightfully for the camera outside the Roselea. Doesn't time fly! The group consisted of Gareth Evans, Eirwen Evans, Sharon Barnard, Corrinne Powell, Julie Williams, Linda Bradley, Susan Bradley and Gareth Barnard.

223. The same venue but a different year of Fochriw trippers to the ever popular Blackpool, this time at the Wakefield Boarding House. Among the holidaymakers are to be seen Willie Thomas, Miss Gittings, Jill Parry, Hetty Evans, Moira Ballard, Ozzie Perry, Minnie Sheen, Sarah Gwen Williams, Will 'Pop' and Eddie Gittings.

224. The streets of Dublin rang to the voices of Fochriw enthusiasts during their trip there in 1951 in support of the Welsh Rugby XV. We believe that the following names are mostly correct but blame the Guinness if there is a difference of opinion! Emlyn Morgan, Gwyn Morgan, Andrew Lynch, Emrys Shankland, Noel Williams, Charlie Hollister, Dai Gittens, Idris Shankland, John Jenkins, Des Evans, John Williams, Jack Thomas and Brian Hodder.

225. An earlier carnival, with carnival queen Pearl Coggan enthroned on the football pitch. Her second-in-command, seated alongside her, is Elizabeth Meade and among the court ladies and pages can be seen Joan Thomas, Rosalind Corcoran, Francis Coles, Miss Perkins, Janet Harding, Eirwen Evans, Paul Davies, Miss Watkins, Nigel Jenkins and Leanne Webber.

226. We finish with a reminiscent photograph of the Welfare Hall, Pantywaun, which provided a well-used venue of entertainment for the village over the years. Here, pictured ouside their Hall, we are fortunate enough to be able to provide the names of many of the adults and children of the community on a day of celebration in 1940. The hall was built by students, had snooker facilities, and was used for a variety of concerts, parties and special events including the well remembered celebration of the end of the war in 1945. In the group are to be seen Jane Williams of Blaen Carno, Mrs Hodges, Tom Jones, Will Bradley of Long Row, Mr and Mrs Richards also of Long Row, Seabourne Williams of Fochriw, Dick Jones, Ann Hughes,Tabatha Smith, Charlie Jones, Elsie and Eddie Farr, Des Thomas who played soccer for Merthyr, Ron Bradley. George Marshalsea, Bronwen Thomas, Ann Jones, Bryn Jones, Vena Thomas, Mr and Mrs Jenkin Richards, Betty Richards, Mary Jane Jones, Tommy 'Halfway' Jones, May Thomas, Jemima Jones, Mary Thomas, Betty Jones, Mr and Mrs Glyn Phillips, Megan Richards, Hadyn Dyer, Roy Thomas, Hady Richards, Eddie Thomas, Gwilfa Thomas who again played soccer for Merthyr Tydfil, Idwal Bradley, Rita Thomas, Maureen Ralph, Elsie Pugh, Mal Hughes, twin brothers Alwyn and Gwyn Bradley, Jean Hughes, Leslie Sorday, Elvet and William Richards and Selwyn Phillips. All names were provided through the excellent memory of Mr Bradley.

Acknowledgements

My sincere thanks go to the following people who so willingly provided me with information, the loan of photographs and data for this publication.

My son Mr Tony Evans, BA., for his superb cartoon depictions, Mrs Geraldine Howells and Mrs Lorraine Brannan of the Rhymney Library for their tremendous interest and support. Mr Lyndon Vaughan, Mrs Iris and Mr Vivian Vaughan, Dr. Steve and Mrs Joanna Jones, The Saint Fagans Museum of Welsh Life, Mr Rees Harris, Mrs Kitty 'The Glwyd' Tibbott, Mrs Mary (Davies) Cooper (Blaina), Mr Cyril Brown, Mr Arnold and Mrs Marina Byles, Mrs Mary Hancock, Mr Elvet Jones (The Ras), Mr Idris Jones (artist of Aberbargoed), Mrs Prudence (Allen) Evans, Mr David and Mrs Lena Jones and daughter Catherine, Mr Bill and Mrs Irene Jones, Mr Clifford Griffiths, Mrs Betty Collier, Mr Gerald and Mrs Valerie Downey (Barry), Mr Trevor Mumford (Tredegar), artist Mrs Olwen Poole Hughes, Mrs Angela Savage (Tredegar), Pastor David John and Mrs Rosalie Williams, Mr Howard and Mrs Eifron Evans (Cardiff), Mr Philip and Mrs Eirwen Jones, Mr Ralph and Mrs Hettie Williams, Miss Julie Williams, Mrs Gwyneira Williams (Ystrad Mynach), Mr J A John (Saundersfoot), Mrs Pat Perry (Abertysswg), Mrs Olwen Savage, Mrs Olive Davies, Mr Lyn Goode, Reverend Philip Jenkins (Swansea), Mrs Olga (Blake) Pearson, Mr Philip Atkinson, Mrs Joan Howells, Mr Neville Andrewartha (Lincoln), Mrs Gwen Parfitt, Mrs Pauline Hatton, Mr Philip Moseley, Mr Tudor Evans, Mr Robert Short (Tredegar), Mr Roy and Mrs Mair Jenkins, Mrs Jean Morgan, Mrs Marina Davies, Mrs Lynne Davies (Abertysswg), Mrs Ann Young (Abertysswg), Mr D Pullen (Abertysswg), Mrs Val Williams (Abertysswg), Mr H Owen (Pontlottyn), Mr Don Harris (Pontlottyn), Mrs Lorraine Watkins (Abertysswg), Mr and Mrs Eric Griffiths, Mr Noel Williams (Fochriw), Mrs Minnie Sheen (Fochriw), Mrs Lilian Evans (Fochriw), Mr Jervis Pearce (Pontlottyn), Mrs Myfanwy Welton, Mrs Nancy Lewis (Newport), Mr Neville and Mrs Annette Shepherd (Abertysswg), Mr John Newton, Mr Will Bradley (Fochriw), Mr Berwyn Jones (Ross-on-Wye), Mr Eric Clayton (Lampeter), Mr Windsor and Mrs Morfa Chapman (Fochriw), Mr Viv Davies, Mrs Margaret James, Mrs Joan Heath, Mrs Heulwen Williams, Mr Paul James (Bargoed), Mrs Margaret Jones. The staff of Bryn Bach Park.

The author would be grateful to hear of any photographs or information that it is felt could be suitably used in further volumes of 'A Portrait of Rhymney'. Contact can be made through Old Bakehouse Publications on telephone number 01495 212600.

Bibliography

Vaynor, A Study of the Welsh Countryside by Elwyn Bowen.
Agricultural Transport in Wales by Geraint Jenkins.
Rhymney Memories by Tom Jones.
Customs and Traditions of Wales by Trevor M Owen.
Echoes of Rhymney by E E Edwards.
Wilkins History of Merthyr by Charles Wilkins.
Beyond the Black Tips by Islwyn Jenkins.
Sowing Beside Still Waters by Brynmor Jones.

For details of further books available in this series please contact the publishers for the latest catalogue.
Send stamp to Old Bakehouse Publications, Church Street, Abertillery, Gwent NP3 1EA.